RELATIONSHIP WITHOUT TEARS

Mopelola Arowosafe

RELATIONSHIP WITHOUT TEARS
Copyright © 2020 by Mopelola Arowosafe

International Standard Book Number: 978-978-56980-7-7
Printed in Nigeria

Cover Designed by:
Speaking Pen International Concept

Forwarded by:
Pastor Belemina Obunge

Published by:
Complete Crown Nigeria Limited
kunlemope1@yahoo.com
completecrownnigltd@gmail.com

keystoafullfillingmarriage@gmail.com
+234 803 343 2764, +234 909 140 8134

Life is all about relationships. While some relationships have positively impacted lives, others have poisoned people's destiny and brought tears of sorrow and suffering.

The author in this book shares on how to enjoy relationship without tears. The combination of scriptural examples and real-life testimonies makes reading very practical and relevant to contemporary times. Without doubt many have fallen prey to deceitful and dangerous relationships that have brought disgrace, dismay and damage to them. The pain is tearing and tormenting. It is with a desire to prevent such troublesome and traumatic experience that Mopelola has put together this thought-provoking work. The beauty of relationship that brings value, builds virtues and begets victorious living is emphasized and encouraged.

As you go through the pages of this wonderful book. It would be clear to you that stimulating communication, strong commitment and spirit-consciousness are vital components of a blessed and blissful **Relationship Without Tears.**
Happy reading!!! Mopelola, congratulations.
Shalom

Belemina OBUNGE
Special Assistant to The General Overseer, and
Pastor in charge of Region, Rivers State, Nigeria.
The Redeemed Christian Church of God

Pastor (Mrs.) Arowosafe

Mopelola has really researched on this book **Relationship Without Tears.** Going through the book, I saw its importance for both the married and singles. The contents are of significance to all form of relationships as it has to do with man and of course, the Almighty God. Do yourself a favour by reading this book and buying for friends and families as you might be saving many relationships, not only marriages from collapse. God bless you.

Pastor Timothy Olaniyan,

PhD; FIPS; FAILGG; FCICN; MNIM; ACIPM;

FBEAN; FCISML; MPM; CSMPC.

Pastor-in-charge, RCCG Lagos Province 12

RECTEM Deputy Rector.

You've got a beautiful piece of write up based on a wonderful idea in your hand.

Pastor Gbadebo Emehiola.

Pastor-in-charge,

RCCG Ogun Province 6

There are books you read that mainly appeal to your mind, filling you with knowledge but no practical views to apply the knowledge acquired. That is why I believe that this book **Relationship Without Tears** will make a remarkable impact in the lives of the readers because it speaks to the spirit, mind and emotion of the reader. This is due to the numerous real-life examples enumerated by Pastor {Mrs} Mopelola Arowosafe.

Pastor Femi Olunuga,
Senior pastor, The Believers Sanctuary,
Ogun state, Nigeria

This book is dedicated to the painful, sweet and heaven's-gain memory of our dear son Oreoluwa Oluwakayode Oluwatimilehin Arowosafe, a very brilliant fourteen-year-old SS2 boy, who slept in the Lord on the 25th of February 2018. We thank God for the privilege we were given to be your parents. God bless your memory.

I quote late Dr Myles Munroe "The value of life is not in its duration, but in its donation.'

CONTENTS

INTRODUCTION

We meet different people at different stages of life. In younger days, when we are in secondary school, college, high school and University, the most important relationship we are thinking of is usually a *love* relationship. So, we tend to believe and relate with the opposite sex in the light and context of *love* relationship and marriage only.

Specifically, I am writing this book to the younger ones to open their eyes to the fact that there are still other types of relationships that can exist between the opposite sex other than marriage. It is also to teach the differences between love, lust, infatuation, healthy and unhealthy relationships. Based on this fact of judging everyone that comes our way in the context of marriage or love, we tend to let some people we meet slip by without appreciating the fact that we might still need them later in the future, either to teach us some vital lesson or to link us to the fulfillment of our purpose. I decided to write on this topic with both biblical and contemporary examples because, I discovered that some of the people we come in contact with are programmed by fate to perform different roles in our lives. I have also grouped relationship into different types based on the impact of such relationships in our lives. To the older ones, I know many of you will relate well with the points I have made because it has either happened to you or to someone you know or you are presently in it. To the younger ones, once again I will like to encourage you to relate well with people you come in contact with so that a healthy relationship that will not bring you tears can exist between you and them. Do not hold tenaciously to any relationship that is not adding value to your life or where your role in each other's life has ended. When there must be a break, simply accept it in good faith and let it go.

As an undergraduate, I met specifically two brothers, Cole and Jade. Brother Cole said God told him I was to be his wife, I replied that I was going to pray about it. During my period of waiting on God for His leading, I told him that we could still be friends. After some weeks he asked me what God told me, he further said that God had reconfirmed to him severally that I would be his wife, I told him that I had not received a positive response or a go-ahead from God. Although still maintaining our friendship, I discovered he had issues with inferiority complex and maturity which were major challenges to me considering the fact that he was not as educated as I was. After some months I told him God was not giving me a go ahead, he became very angry and annoyed with me. He said and I quote *"God has told me that you are proud, you are stubborn and arrogant but you are deceiving yourself because it is you I will marry"*. He harassed, insulted and frustrated me. He kept mounting pressure on me, but I made sure the relationship remained platonic between us, but after about a year he fought with me and finally stopped seeing me and returned to his base in another state, different from the state where my school was located. Fourteen years after he had left angrily, and I had already gotten married, Brother Cole called me on phone that he wanted to see me. My surprise was better imagined, I told my husband and he said we should go and see him, so we went and met him in our office already waiting for us. He said he needed my assistance and I asked him how he got my number, he said he met somebody in the state where I resided with my family who told him that I was close to the man he needed help from. By the time he finished narrating the story of the journey of his life, we felt very sorry for him and of course my husband helped him.

After that incident, I began to have this belief that it was possible God spoke to him about me, but the message was not on marriage. Why I started having that feeling was because the costly mistake he made that brought him from a very top position to that level was a thing that anybody close to me would not venture into, because naturally I have this instinct about how that particular issue will always end. Everyone close to me will always hear it in my speech and in my approach towards life and success that I don't and won't allow such a thing to happen to people around me. I thought within me that probably if we had remained friends and not parted with quarrel because I said I was not going to marry him, just maybe he would not have gotten into that mess he found himself and family (he was already married with children).

Brother Jade was an engineering student I met while I was an undergraduate in a Nigerian University; he later became a family friend. He also felt I could be his wife; he kept following my spiritual growth and progress, kept encouraging me to pray about my marital life and, later proposed by telling me that he felt God was leading him to me. I told him after I had prayed that God was not giving me a go-ahead to start a relationship with him. He did not argue with my response, so we remained friends. After our individual programmes in the University, we parted. We met again some eleven years later. I had married my own husband and he also had married his sweetheart. His family wanted to relocate to the state where my family and I resided, so we got connected again and my family eventually helped them in a little way to ensure their relocating and settling down was easy and fast.

I knew Mr. Tony while at the University who was in a relationship with Miss Ella. They were living together, and were always seen together hanging around each other in an intimate and steaming manner. They were like an example of love. Years after, I met the lady and was surprised that she and the guy were not married. During the course of our discussion, I discovered that the relationship was just based on lust and infatuation and not true love. Unfortunately, at the time of our discussion, she was living in regret because she said she saw some signs that showed that her relationship was not true love, but she ignored them.

The three stories narrated above and more that happened in my University days which will be narrated in this book were part of what prompted me to write on these issues of friendship, relationship and why we meet different people in our journey through life. We meet different people for different reasons; we must identify the reason(s), but most importantly learn whatever lesson God wants us to learn from the relationship. I have always believed and said that life is a cycle; we meet some people when we are down, and on our way up we might meet again or need each other's help. We may never meet others again but they would have succeeded in imparting knowledge and values into our lives which can never be forgotten in a hurry. If the part of the persons you met has ended in your life and they leave, don't hold it against them, because leaving does not make them bad persons. It simply means their part has ended in that chapter of your life. Never beg any one to stay with you in any relationship, if you do, they will frustrate you, dictate the pace and eventually leave you hurt with a scar or permanently maimed. I will encourage you to read diligently as the Holy Spirit teaches us about different types of relationships and their characteristics using biblical and contemporary examples to show the differences between healthy and unhealthy relationships that will determine if it will bring you joy or tears.

Mopelola Arowosafe
Bestselling Author of *'Keys to a Fulfilling Marriage'*

CHAPTER 1

Relationships that Teach Vital Lessons of Life
"Learn all You Must"

Relationship develops for different reasons. Sometimes we are brought together by divine arrangement, circumstances or providence. It therefore implies that as a single sister or brother you must realize that it is not everyone you meet or that is nice to you that you can marry. Some people we meet today are for the purpose of our tomorrow. The influence of a relationship is powerful and more often than not, unappreciated especially if it is a negative occurrence. Whether we realize it or not, relationships that we've had or are into have shaped or are shaping our lives to be who we are today or who we will become tomorrow.

Contemporary and Biblical Examples

Judah and Tamar
"And Judah took a wife for Er his firstborn, whose name was Tamar.
And Er, Judah's firstborn, was wicked in the sight of the LORD; and the LORD slew him.
And Judah said unto Onan, go in unto thy brother's wife, and marry her, and raise up seed to thy brother.
And Onan knew that the seed should not be his; and it came to pass, when he went in unto his brother's wife, that he spilled it on the ground, lest that he should give seed to his brother.
And the thing which he did displeased the LORD: wherefore he slew him also". Gen. 38:6-10

Tamar was married to Judah's first born, who God decided to kill by Himself not because of what Tamar did or did not do but because he was wicked. According to custom Tamar was again married to her late husband's younger brother, not according to her will but according to tradition. Onan decided he did not want to follow tradition by getting Tamar pregnant and naming the child in the memory of his late elder brother so God decided to kill him too. Judah must have felt that probably something was wrong with Tamar, so that his last and only child would not be killed by her again. He deceived her, by asking her to go to her father's house and continue to mourn with a promise that when his last son was old enough, he would marry her.

"Then said Judah to Tamar his daughter in law, remain a widow at thy father's house, till Shelah my son be grown: for he said, lest peradventure he dies also, as his brethren did. And Tamar went and dwelt in her father's house". Gen. 38:11.

Tamar waited and continued mourning, still holding unto the promise of marriage between her and Shelah by Judah her father-in-law. Years after, she kept waiting until she discovered that Shelah was already a grown man but she was not given to him to marry.

"...for she saw that Shelah was grown, and she was not given unto him to wife". Gen. 38:14c

Tamar decided to take the bull by the horns, and take her destiny in her hands. We should not forget that no man will likely want to marry her because she would have been labeled as a husband killer, and she was not getting younger. She heard that her father-in-law who just finished mourning his wife was on his way to his farm. Tamar removed her mourning clothes, dressed like a harlot and stayed by the road where Judah would be passing.

"And in process of time the daughter of Shuah Judah's wife died; and Judah was comforted, and went up unto his sheepshearers to Timnath, he and his friend Hirah the Adullamite.

And it was told Tamar, saying, behold thy father in law goeth up to Timnath to shear his sheep.

And she put her widow's garments off from her, and covered her with a vail, and wrapped herself, and sat in an open place, which is by the way to Timnath; for she saw that Shelah was grown, and she was not given unto him to wife.

When Judah saw her, he thought her to be an harlot; because she had covered her face". Gen. 38:12-15

For the first time, life had thrown at Tamar the opportunity to make her own choice and bargain her future. The adversity and misfortune of the past taught her to be thick-skinned and to know that success does not usually happen by chance but by deliberate, calculated risk and action. Tamar allowed Judah to have sex with her and she got from him evidences that could be used to prove his ownership of the pregnancy. After some months she was found pregnant and those who had been unfaithful in keeping their own side of the bargain and agreement were ready to burn her for committing "adultery"

"And it came to pass about three months after, that it was told Judah, saying, Tamar thy daughter in law hath played the harlot; and also, behold, she is with child by whoredom. And Judah said, bring her forth, and let her be burnt.

When she was brought forth, she sent to her father in law, saying, By the man, whose these are, am I with child: and she said, Discern, I pray thee, whose are these, the signet, and bracelets, and staff.

And Judah acknowledged them, and said, she hath been more righteous than I; because that I gave her not to Shelah my son. And he knew her again no more." Gen. 38:24-26

Tamar's situation must have taught her that things don't just happen in life; you have to make it happen. Tamar eventually gave birth to a set of twins, one of which was mentioned in the lineage of Jesus Christ as His great grandfather.

"And it came to pass in the time of her travail, that, behold, twins were in her womb.

And it came to pass, when she travailed, that the one put out his hand: and the midwife took and bound upon his hand a scarlet thread, saying, this came out first,

And it came to pass, as he drew back his hand, that, behold, his brother came out: and she said, how hast thou broken forth? this breach be upon thee: therefore, his name was called Pharez.

And afterward came out his brother, that had the scarlet thread upon his hand: and his name was called Zarah." Gen. 38:27-30.

"The book of the generation of Jesus Christ, the son of David, the son of Abraham.

3

Abraham begat Isaac; and Isaac begat Jacob; and Jacob begat Judas and his brethren;

And Judas begat Phares and Zara of Thamar; and Phares begat Esrom; and Esrom begat Aram; And Aram begat Aminadab; and Aminadab begat Naasson; and Naasson begat Salmon;

And Salmon begat Booz of Rachab; and Booz begat Obed of Ruth; and Obed begat Jesse;

And Jesse begat David the king; and David the king begat Solomon of her that had been the wife of Urias; And Solomon begat Roboam; and Roboam begat Abia; and Abia begat Asa;

And Asa begat Josaphat; and Josaphat begat Joram; and Joram begat Ozias;

And Ozias begat Joatham; and Joatham begat Achaz; and Achaz begat Ezekias;

And Ezekias begat Manasses; and Manasses begat Amon; and Amon begat Josias;

And Josias begat Jechonias and his brethren, about the time they were carried away to Babylon: And after they were brought to Babylon, Jechonias begat Salathiel; and Salathiel begat Zorobabel; And Zorobabel begat Abiud; and Abiud begat Eliakim; and Eliakim begat Azor; And Azor begat Sadoc; and Sadoc begat Achim; and Achim begat Eliud;

And Eliud begat Eleazar; and Eleazar begat Matthan; and Matthan begat Jacob;

And Jacob begat Joseph the husband of Mary, of whom was born Jesus, who is called Christ". Matt. 1:1-16

When I was in secondary school, Senior Sade was in my dormitory in the boarding house. She was very saucy and abusive, she cursed any one that crossed her path. This made even young men afraid of her: She consequently became jealous and envious of any lady whom a young man asked out. If she got to know, then the lady was in trouble. Senior Sade was saucy and uncultured. One day, a young man asked me out, I told him I was not interested in going into a relationship with him. Senior Sade got to know and after sometime I just noticed that whenever I passed by, I would hear a snide remark like "foolish I am ready" or "nonsensical I am ready" from other students. I did not know I was the one they were referring to until a year after she finished from the school and one of her group members asked me if I knew I was the one they were referring to as "foolish I am ready" and "nonsensical I am ready" I said no but in any case I asked her what it meant. She told me that Senior Sade told them I went back to the young man I refused to go into a love relationship with and told him I was ready for a relationship. My anger could just be better imagined but after a while I decided I wanted to know the source of the false story. I went to Senior Sade's house during the holiday and she said a senior who had also left the school told her I said it. Fortunately, the person in question had a younger one in my school, whom I sent to her sister during another holiday only for her to say another senior who had left the school said it. The incident made me to realize that it was possible for people to cook up a lie against another person. This incident has helped me as a leader because in this case only myself and few other people who knew the kind of person I was knew that the story was false, so if someone says he or she is not lying about an allegation leveled against him or her and my spirit is not in doubt then I will believe the person. I also learnt that the fury of jealousy can only be better imagined.

"And it came to pass after these things, that his master's wife cast her eyes upon Joseph; and she said, lie with me. But he refused, and said unto his master's wife, Behold, my master wotteth not what is with me in the house, and he hath committed all that he hath to my hand; There is none greater in this house than I; neither hath he kept back anything from me but thee, because thou art his wife: how then can I do this great wickedness, and sin against God? And it came pass, as she spake with Joseph day by day, that he hearkened not unto her, to lie by her, or to be with her. And it came to pass about this time, that Joseph went into the house to do his business; and there was none of the men of the house there within. And she caught him by his garment saying, lie with me: and he left his garment in her hand, and fled, and got him out. And it came to pass, when she saw that he had left his garment in her hand, and was fled forth. That she called unto the men of her house, and spake unto them, saying, See, he hath brought in an Hebrew unto us to mock us; he came in unto me to lie with me, and I cried with a loud voice: And it came to pass, when he heard that I lifted up my voice

and cried, that he left his garment with me, and fled, and got him out. And she laid up his garment by her, until his Lord came home. And she spake unto him according to these words, saying, the Hebrew servant, which thou hast brought unto us, came in unto me to mock me; And it came to pass, as I lifted up my voice and cried, that he left his garment with me, and fled out. And it came to pass, when his master heard the words of his wife, which she spake unto him, saying, after this manner did thy servant to me; that his wrath was kindled. And Joseph's master took him, and put him into the prison, a place where the king's prisoners were bound: and he was there in the prison." Gen. 39:7-20.

Relationship that we make can also give us vital life skills; like sharpening our mind, knowing ourselves better and becoming more inspired to reach our goals and advancing our career. While on Industrial Training in a multinational company in the course of her programme at the polytechnic, Tola told me she met a young, brilliant and handsome Deji who wanted to marry her. She was not ready for an emotional relationship but they remained friends. Deji was already climbing the ladder to the top at a very young age. Tola said she learnt some things from Deji that eventually changed her career focus. She noticed there were a lot of older people who were subordinate to Deji and out of curiosity she asked him why it was so and he told her that it was due to the type of certificate they possessed. This was an eye opener for her because she decided to tread academically as he advised. She also said she learnt that anything you want to achieve is better achieved when you are still young. Deji felt they were meant to marry but she knew they met to give her the needed focus in life, broaden her mind and inspire her to aim and go for the best in life.

Michael Jordan was born in 1963 in the slums of Brooklyn, New York. He had four siblings and his father's earnings were not sufficient to provide for the whole family. He grew up in a poor neighborhood. Exposed to mindless violence and heavy discrimination in the slums, he saw for himself only a hopeless future. His father saw in Michael a lost soul and decided to do something. He gave the 13years old Michael, a piece of used clothing and asked: "What do you think the value of this outfit would be?" Jordan replied, "Maybe one dollar". His father said, "Can you sell it for two dollars? If you can sell it, it would mean that you are a big help to your family. Jordan nodded his head, saying" I'll try, but no guarantee that I'll be successful". Jordan carefully washed the cloth, because they didn't have an iron, to smoothen the cloth he leveled it with clothes brush on a flat board, and kept it in the sun to dry. The next day he brought the cloth to a crowded underground station. After offering it for more than six hours, Jordan finally managed to sell it for two dollars. He took the two-dollar bill and ran home. After that, every day he looked for used clothing, washed and ironed it, and sold it in the crowd. More than ten days later his father gave him a piece of used clothing, "can you think of a way you can sell this for 20 bucks?" Aghast Jordan said "How is it possible?" this outfit can only fetch two dollars at the most. His father replied "why don't you try it first, there might be a way." After racking his brains for few hours, Jordan finally got an idea. He asked for his cousin's help to paint a picture of Donald Duck and Mickey Mouse on the garment. Then he tried to sell it in the school where the children of the rich studied. Soon a house keeper, who was there to pick his master, bought that outfit for his master. The master was only a little boy of 10years. He loved it so much he gave a five-dollar tip. "25 dollars was a huge amount for Jordan, the equivalent of a month's salary of his father. When he got home, his father gave him yet another piece of used clothing. "Are you able to resell at a price of 200 dollars" Jordan's eyes lit up. This time Jordan accepted the cloths without the slightest doubt. Two months later, a popular movie actress from the movie "Charlie's Angels", Farah Fawcett came to New York for her movie promo. After the press conference, Jordan made his way through the security forces to reach the side of Farah Fawcett and requested her autograph on the piece of clothing. When Fawcett saw the innocent boy asking for her autograph, she gladly signed it. Jordan was shouting very excitedly "This is the jersey signed by Miss Farah Fawcett, the selling price is 1200 dollars, and he auctioned off the clothes, to a businessman for a price of 1200 dollars. Upon returning home, his father broke into tears and said "I am amazed that you really did it my child! You're really great". That night, Jordan slept alongside his father. His father asked "Son, in your experience selling these three pieces of clothing, what did you learn about success? Jordan replied, "Where there's a will, there's a way". His father nodded "What you say is not entirely wrong. But that was not my intention. I just wanted to show you that if a piece of clothing which is worth only a dollar can also be increased in value, then how about us living and thinking humans? We may be darker and poorer but what if we can increase our value? Our potential is so great, and should not be viewed small and low only because of our status, looks or wealth. Even a diamond is just a stone before it has been polished. Keep improving yourself trying your best and striving ahead." This thought enlightened young Jordan, even a piece of used clothing could be made dignified, then why not me? There is absolutely no reason to underestimate myself. From then on, Michael Jordan felt that his future would be beautiful and full of hope. He went on to become the greatest basketball player of all times with a net worth of 1.7billion USD [2019].

This is another story told by one of my mentors and I quote:
"When things were great, I would say that every weekend in my house was a hive of activities. Friends, well-wishers and associates were always around and we all just enjoyed ourselves after hard work for the week. The bar in my living room was always replenished with choice wines while the resident cook was always on hand to entertain my friends. However, I cannot count up to three of those friends that are still around me today. A particular incident opened my eyes and forced me to meditate on many things in life. I had paid a visit to a friend who always invited me to his living room and bring out assorted drink and food anytime I was at his house. I decided to visit him when things were very rough for me. The moment he sighted me; he told his gateman to ask me to wait for him outside. He, eventually, came out and barely said hello before heading for the car… driving off. I was shaken by the experience. It happened at my lowest point in life. I decided to give up on everything, and tried to commit suicide. After unsuccessful suicide attempts, I decided to take to medications and tried to understand the laws of life. It was at that time that a Christian group invited me to a gathering where other people were sharing their life experiences. Their experiences were worse than what I wanted to commit suicide over. My confidence grew as a result of my encounter with the group. I got the courage to revive my company. I was able to sit at my desk to redesign

the strategy for my company and life." This is the experience of one of my mentors who is doing very well now as a foremost industrialist.

I once heard the story of an executive who was billed to travel to Lagos in Nigeria from his base at Port Harcourt. He had planned that if his driver got to his place by 9:00am in the morning; they could set out for the airport and could meet up with his 10 o'clock flight to Lagos. He dressed up around 8:45am, and waited for his driver of over ten years who had never been late in keeping to time. However, his driver was nowhere to be found. The driver later showed up at 9:25am. The executive was enraged, he rained abuses on the driver, hopped into his car and instructed the driver to hurry to the airport to see if he could make it to the airport on time. As he entered the airport area, he noticed that a plane was taxing to the runway, preparing to take off. The executive became even angrier with his driver. He realized that he would not meet-up with his 12noon appointment in Lagos. Some 20minutes after the take-off, while he waited for another plane, an announcement was made that the plane he missed, had crashed. The man was speechless. He headed for the car park, located his driver, entered his car and asked the driver to return to his house. He did not utter a word. At home, after spending some time to glorify God, he took his driver to the nearest super market and asked him to pick anything he (the driver) wanted, while he continued to chant, "You are my saviour." He learnt the power of the Supreme Being in the ruling and directing affairs of the life of mortals.

I was touched by the testimony of the wife of one of my mentors. She openly confessed that her husband has turned her from a woman who had no appetite for intellectual work to a woman whose hobby is now reading. In her words: "Before I met my husband and even in the early days of our relationship, I was always quarrelling with him over what I called excessive intellectual adventure. I thought the role of a woman was in the kitchen but my husband changed that. Anytime he bought a book he would ask me to read and he would create time for us to discuss lessons from the book. Over time, I have become increasingly fascinated with seeking knowledge. Today I represent him at events he cannot attend personally".

My mentor shared this tip with me: "Most men who get busy with being successful without carrying their wives along are digging their graves. If you fail to upgrade your wife at the time you should, when crisis comes, you may not survive it because there is no cushion at home to fall on.

I was told about a man who when he first started his comic magazine, had encountered an individual who appeared to him as the Messiah he was looking for. The man was to assist him in the production of the magazine. The man had assured him that he was a close friend of a popular printer in Ibadan, Oyo State, Nigeria. He believed him and all the initial money he had gathered from different sources were handed over to him. As he was writing, he was handing over the copy to him and the man would always bring the same layout to him when he expected him to be advancing towards the final copy of the magazine. He decided to pay a surprise visit to the printer and he nearly fainted when he discovered that the man assisting him had not paid the printer any money. He had defrauded him of his money. The man vanished once he knew the game was up. That meant all the money he had saved for the project's take-off was gone. He could have given-up but he refused to do that because he was clear as to where he was taking the project to and the benefits of accomplishing it. He decided to look for ways out of the mess. He eventually got in touch with the owner of the press who confirmed that the person in question was a serial conman who had defrauded quite a number of people. Out of sympathy, the owner of the printing press printed for him on credit at a subsidized rate and allowed him to pay as he sold the magazine. Thank God they were able to take off with that arrangement. He learnt the power of resilience and courage.

CHAPTER 2

Relationships That Make Your Heart Melt and Your Head Spin
"Open Your Eyes and Use Your Brain"

In this type of relationship reality doesn't usually count; it is based on your feelings. You meet this man or lady and he/she sweeps you off your feet, your heart melts and it is love at first sight. You have this feeling of I can't live without this person, this relationship causes you to float and have a feeling of it being pure and made from heaven. You close your eyes and block your ears to anything negative; you tend to hate whoever is against or advises against such relationship. Unfortunately, most people in this type of relationship equate their feeling of lust and infatuation to real love.

Biblical and Contemporary Examples
Jacob and Rachel

> *"And Jacob loved Rachel and said, I will serve thee seven years for Rachel thy younger daughter. <u>And Jacob served seven years for Rachel, and they seemed unto him but a few days. For the love he had to her;</u> Gen.29:18&20   – Emphasis added.*

Things to Note About This Type of Relationship
- **It is usually a shadow of the real thing to come**:
  It is not the real thing but surprisingly a lot of people usually cling to the shadow without knowing it because it looks so real.

- **It brings trouble on the long run to the parties involved**

> *"And Laban went to shear his sheep: and Rachel had stolen the images that were her father's" – Gen. 31:19*

"With whomsoever thou findest thy gods let him not live: before our brethren discern thou what is thine with me, and take it to thee. For Jacob knew not that Rachel had stolen them. Now Rachel had taken the images and put them in the camel's furniture, and sat upon them. And Laban searched all the tent, but found them not. And she said to her father, let it not displease my lord that I cannot rise up before thee, for the custom of women is upon me. And he searched but found not the images" Gen. 31:32, 34-35.

- **Sense of reasoning is lost in this type of relationship because the object of admiration is loved beyond reasoning**.

I heard of a lady who got impregnated by her boyfriend and when she discussed with the man, he started crying that they were not financially ready to shoulder the responsibility of a child. Based on excuse that he 'loved' her, he suggested that the lady should abort the pregnancy. The lady argued that they keep the baby because they were planning to get married, but the man pleaded that if the lady loved him as he loved her then she would abort the pregnancy. She aborted the first pregnancy and funny enough there was a second and a third abortion which the lady did because she *"loved"* her boyfriend necessitating serial abortions (Love is not stupid and it is not selfish). Both of them had forgotten that true love seeks the joy of the partner first and not his own. The man did not eventually marry this lady after three successive abortions.

I knew a lady back then on campus that had a lustful relationship with a cult guy and they were cohabiting. Woes betide her when her boyfriend returned from his cult meeting late at night and did not meet her at home. When he met her at home, he would beat her black and blue, after which he would rape her, eat and sleep off while the lady cried and nursed her wounds. The next morning, he would wake up sober and start crying that he loved her and that if she left him, his life would not be complete. The lady believed him. Her friends advised her to leave him before he killed her, but she always told her friends that she loved him and he loved her. She added that her boyfriend was just under pressure. She said that when he was not under the influence of alcohol, he was a good man, who promised to stop abusing her, till she left school, her boyfriend did not change. Nemesis eventually caught up with him because of the cult activities and the lady was left with a low self-esteem and a battered image.

- **It is not God's perfect choice:**
  "And when the Lord saw that Leah was hated, he opened her womb; but Rachel was barren" Gen. 29:31;

In my own opinion, Rachel was not God's perfect will for Jacob in marriage; God intends that marriage between one man and one woman. As a result of Jacob's love for Rachel, he violated God's word to become the first person to marry two women legally in the Bible. I also believe that the coming of Messiah through the lineage of Leah and not Rachael is symbolic, significant and worthy of note

"Abraham begat Isaac; and Isaac begat Jacob; and Jacob begat Judas and his brethren;
And Judas begat Phares and Zara of Thamar; and Phares begat Esrom; and Esrom begat Aram; And Aram begat Aminadab; and Aminadab begat Naasson; and Naasson begat Salmon; And Salmon begat Booz of Rachab; and Booz begat Obed of Ruth; and Obed begat Jesse; And Jesse begat David the king; and David the king begat Solomon of he that had been the wife of Urias; And Solomon begat Roboam; and Roboam begat Abia; and Abia begat Asa; And Asa begat Josaphat; and Josaphat begat Joram; and Joram begat Ozias; And Ozias begat Joatham; and Joatham begat Achaz; and Achaz begat Ezekias; And Ezekias begat Manasses; and Manasses begat Amon; and Amon begat Josias; And Josias begat Jechonias and his brethren, about the time they were carried away to Babylon: And after they were brought to Babylon, Jechonias begat Salathiel; and Salathiel begat Zorobabel;
And Zorobabel begat Abiud; and Abiud begat Eliakim; and Eliakim begat Azor;

And Azor begat Sadoc; and Sadoc begat Achim; and Achim begat Eliud;
And Eliud begat Eleazar; and Eleazar begat Matthan; and Matthan begat Jacob;
And Jacob begat Joseph the husband of Mary, of whom was born Jesus, who is called Christ." Matt. 1:2-16

Leah was also buried with the patriarchs while Rachel was not. This also is a message about God's choice which most times is not our choice. Ultimately His [God] choice is always the best.

And he charged them, and said unto them, I am to be gathered unto my people: bury me with my fathers in the cave that is in the field of Ephron the Hittite,
In the cave that is in the field of Machpelah, which is before Mamre, in the land of Canaan, which Abraham bought with the field of Ephron the Hittite for a possession of a burying place.
There they buried Abraham and Sarah his wife; there they buried Isaac and Rebekah his wife; and there I buried Leah. Gen. 49:29-31.

"And Rachel died, and was buried in the way to Ephrath, which is Bethlehem." Gen. 35:19

Helen met Jake in their University days. He was tall, slim, handsome, smooth talking, caring, with laughing eyes, winning ways, he knew how to make a lady melt in his company and she fell in love with him immediately. Unlike Jake who was wise in the ways of the world, Helen was an innocent girl.

Everybody told her men like Jake do not make good husbands. She refused to listen because Jake always knew the right time to send gifts and take her out. He knew the right words to say to her, never shouted at her, he was always composed and in control. Towards their final year in school, Jake met another girl and left Helen. Helen nearly died because she felt it was the end of her world. Many years after Helen had married, she met Jake, still with his smooth talking, smiling and unruffled act. He almost swept her off her feet again, nearly causing her to abandon her marriage.

- **Men in this type of relationship do not usually settle down to marry.**
In relationships terms, they are referred to as playboys. In the church, brothers like this will not propose but the way they attach themselves to other ladies can make their fiancée jealous. They waste the time of any lady that mistakenly cling to their affection because such a lady will likely wait forever, just like Helen in the story above.

- **The men/ladies involved do not usually have genuine relationship with God.**
"And Laban went to shear his sheep; and Rachel had stolen <u>the images</u> that were her fathers" – Gen. 31:19

What did Rachel the wife of Jacob, a man with the covenant of God upon his life, want to do with the images of a foreign god (a god that needs to be carried from place to place)?
"And the LORD said unto Jacob, return unto the land of thy fathers, and to thy kindred; and I will be with thee." Gen. 31:3
This tells us that she had not fully embraced the God of Jacob. Such people are Christians that can easily blend with the church and the world; they are good actors and actresses, with one leg in the church and the other in the world.
"And now, though thou wouldest needs be gone, because thou sore longest after thy father's house, yet wherefore has thou stolen my gods? Gen. 31: 30

Rachel was a smooth talker and a liar. People in this category are very good at lying, their tongues talk very smoothly, they are master planners and schemers that even if you are about to catch them, they sleekly slip out of your grip.
"So Laban went into Jacob's tent and into Leah's tent and into the tent of two maidservants, but he found nothing. After he

came out of Leah's tent, he entered Rachel's tent. Now Rachel had taken the household gods and put them inside her camel's saddle and was sitting on them. Laban searched through everything in the tent but found nothing. <u>Rachel said to her father "don't be angry, my lord, that I cannot stand up in your presence; I am having my period." So he searched but could not find the house hold gods.</u>" Gen. 31:33-35[NIV version]

"With whomsoever thou findest thy gods, let him not live: before our brethren discern thou, what is thine with me, and take it to thee, for Jacob knew not that Rachel had stolen them" Gen.31: 32

"And this is the condemnation, that light is come into the world, and men loved darkness rather than light, because their deeds were evil.
For every one that doeth evil hateth the light, neither cometh to the light, lest his deeds should be reproved.
But he that doeth truth cometh to the light, that his deeds may be made manifest, that they are wrought in God." John 3:19-21

"And the Lord said unto Jacob, return unto the land of thy fathers, and to thy kindred; and I will be with thee" Gen. 31:3

God told Jacob to leave the house of Laban, that He the living and mighty God was going to be with him. Jacob was a man that had a relationship with God, yet Rachel still held unto the gods of her father for protection. She was a chameleon. A relationship where you don't share the same faith and belief will always bring problem and forever a thorn in your flesh with free-flowing tears accompanying. The Bible states

"Can two walk together, except they be agreed?" Amos 3:3

"Be ye not unequally yoked together with unbelievers: for what fellowship hath righteousness with unrighteousness? And what communion hath light with darkness? And what concord hath

Christ with Belial? Or what part hath he that believeth with an infidel? And what agreement hath the temple of God with idols? For ye are the temple of the living God; as God hath said, I will dwell in them, and walk in them; and I will be their God, and they shall be my people. Wherefore come out from among them, and be ye separate, saith the Lord, and touch not the unclean thing; and I will receive you" II Cor. 6:14-17

"This then is the message which he have heard of him, and declare unto you, that God is light and in him is no darkness at all. If we say that we have fellowship with him, and walk in darkness, we lie and do not the truth" – I John 1:5-6

- **Men in this type of relationship waste your time:**
  On account of not wanting to be seen as a bad person, they usually don't come out straight to say that they are no longer interested in the relationship. They want to subtly leave or frustrate you, and they always want you to see them as the good person while you are the one that is not patient enough even after so many years of dating. They never say it is over. They are never in a hurry because they actually don't have anywhere they are going; they are like pendulum, moving back and forth with no destination in view.

Samson and Delilah

"And it came to pass afterward, that <u>he loved a woman</u> in the valley of Sorek, whose name was Delilah.
And the lords of the Philistines came up unto her, and said unto her, Entice him, and see wherein his great strength lieth, and by what means we may prevail against him, that we may bind him to afflict him: and we will give thee every one of us eleven hundred pieces of silver.
And Delilah said to Samson, <u>tell me, I pray thee, wherein thy great strength lieth, and wherewith thou mightest be bound to afflict thee.</u>

And Samson said unto her, if they bind me with seven green withs that were never dried, then shall I be weak, and be as another man.

Then the lords of the Philistines brought up to her seven green withs which had not been dried, and she bound him with them.

Now there were men lying in wait, abiding with her in the chamber. And she said unto him, The Philistines be upon thee, Samson. And he brake the withs, as a thread of tow is broken when it toucheth the fire. So his strength was not known.

And Delilah said unto Samson, Behold, thou hast mocked me, and told me lies: now tell me, I pray thee, wherewith thou mightest be bound.

And he said unto her, if they bind me fast with new ropes that never were occupied, then shall I be weak, and be as another man.

Delilah therefore took new ropes, and bound him therewith, and said unto him, The Philistines be upon thee, Samson. And there were liars in wait abiding in the chamber. And he brake them from off his arms like a thread.

And Delilah said unto Samson, hitherto thou hast mocked me, and told me lies: tell me wherewith thou mightest be bound. And he said unto her, If thou weavest the seven locks of my head with the web.

And she fastened it with the pin, and said unto him, The Philistines be upon thee, Samson. And he awaked out of his sleep, and went away with the pin of the beam, and with the web.

And she said unto him, how canst thou say, I love thee, when thine heart is not with me? thou hast mocked me these three times, and hast not told me wherein thy great strength lieth.

And it came to pass, when she pressed him daily with her words, and urged him, so that his soul was vexed unto death;

That he told her all his heart, and said unto her. There hath not come a razor upon mine head; for I have been a Nazarite unto God from my mother's womb: if I be shaven, then my strength will go from me, and I shall become weak, and be like any other man.

And when Delilah saw that he had told her all his heart, she sent and called for the lords of the Philistines, saying, come up this once, for he hath shewed me all his heart. Then the lords of the Philistines came up unto her, and brought money in their hand.

And she made him sleep upon her knees; and she called for a man, and she caused him to shave off the seven locks of his head; and she began to afflict him, and his strength went from him.
And she said, The Philistines be upon thee, Samson. And he awoke out of his sleep, and said, I will go out as at other times before, and shake myself. And he wist not that the LORD was departed from him.
But the Philistines took him, and put out his eyes, and brought him down to Gaza, and bound him with fetters of brass; and he did grind in the prison house." Judges 16:4-21. [Emphasis added]

Samson loved Delilah. Like the earlier examples, Delilah swept Samson off his feet so much that he could not differentiate between lust, infatuation and the voice of reasoning. I am sure all through the period she was tempting him to know his source of power, Samson's heart would have been telling him to run but like everyone in this type of relationship. He didn't run until he landed in big or irreversible trouble. Delilah asked Samson for the source of his power the first time,

  "And Delilah said to Samson, tell me, I pray thee, wherein thy great strength lieth and wherewith though mightest be bound to afflict thee" Judges 16:6.

What kind of love will make a man joke with the fact that the woman he loves wants to know how he could be bound and afflicted so that she could reveal the secrets to his enemy?

When I was in the University, Mr. Tiger told a decent Christian lady, Miss Lillian he was going to marry her someday. One day Mr. Tiger was holding his lover girl, Miss Foolish while walking along the road with her hanging on him, they met Miss Lillian. In Mr. Tiger's usual manner he called Miss Lillian his wife, Miss Lillian replied that he was already holding unto his wife Mr. Tiger replied, pointing to Miss Foolish who he was holding and said; "She knows I can never marry her because her type of girl is bad that if any mother sets eyes on her, she will faint because she knows the life of her son is ruined". The lover girl that was referred to as being too bad and promiscuous to be a wife to any man because she was just good enough to be a *sex partner* or *sin partner* was listening to the conversation but still clung to Mr. Tiger smiling because she loved him. Like Delilah, Mr. Tiger boldly said it to Miss Foolish that she was too bad for marriage, yet, she took it as a joke.

Delilah did not stop at asking Samson the source of his power and how he could be afflicted but practically carried out all the responses of Samson by calling the enemies on him, yet after the first episode Samson did not run. Delilah asked the second and the third time and like the first time, she called the enemies to validate the truth of his claims and yet there was still a fourth time, perhaps, Samson should have asked her that if the first answer was the truth and the enemies came upon him as she called them and his power was taken away or destroyed, what would she do with the remains of his powerless body or what would become of him and his God ordained purpose to the children of Israel? Unfortunately; he never did.

> *"And she said unto him, how canst thou say, I love thee, when thine heart is not with me? Thou hast mocked me these three times and hast not told me where in thy great strength lieth".*
>
> *"And it came to pass, when she pressed him daily with her words, and urged him, so that his soul was vexed unto death: that he told her all his heart, and said unto her, there hath not come a razor upon mine head for I have been a Nazarite unto God from my mother's womb: if I be shaven, then my strength will go from me, and I shall become weak like any other man"*
> *Judges 16: 16-17.*

Samson threw caution to the wind and poured out his heart to Delilah. Delilah had a mission, People like Delilah are very persistent and if you don't run like Joseph did, your life and purpose would be destroyed. Just like before, Delilah called the enemy to validate the truth, but it turned out to be true and this was what led Samson to the beginning of the end, unlike before, this time around it was a journey of no return because it was no longer a joke. What a tragedy!

> *"And she made him sleep upon her knees; and she called for a man and she caused him to shave off the seven locks of his head: and she began to afflict him, and his strength went from him. And she said, the Philistines be upon thee, Samson. And he awake out of his sleep and said, I will go out as at other times before and shake myself. And he wist not that the LORD was*

departed from him; but the Philistines took him, and put out his eyes, and brought him down to Gaza, and bound him with fetters of brass and he did grind in the prison house" Judges 16:19-21.

What a tragic end to a mighty man who could not differentiate between love and lust.

Tamar and Amnon

" And it came to pass after this, that Absalom the son of David had a fair sister, whose name was Tamar; and <u>Amnon the son of David loved her</u>. And Amnon was so vexed, that he fell sick for his sister Tamar; for she was a virgin; and Amnon thought it hard for him to do anything to her. But Amnon had a friend, whose name was Jonadab, the son of Shimeah David's brother: and Jonadab was a very subtil man. And he said unto him, why art thou, being the king's son, lean from day to day? wilt thou not tell me? And Amnon said unto him, <u>I love Tamar</u>, my brother Absalom's sister". 2 Samuel13: 1-4

Like the other examples, there is always the continuous use and repetition of the word 'love. Amnon claimed he loved Tamar so much that he became sick and obsessed with his love for her.

- **Pretense and deceit are one of the characteristics of men/ladies in this type or relationship**

   Like the previously mentioned examples men/ladies in this type of relationship live a pretentious and deceitful life

"So Amnon lay down, and made himself sick: and when the king was come to see him, Amnon said unto the king, I pray thee, let Tamar my sister come, and make me a couple of cakes in my sight, that I may eat at her hand. Then David sent home to Tamar, saying, Go now to thy brother Amnon's house, and dress him meat. So Tamar went to her brother Amnon's house; and he was laid down. And she took flour, and kneaded it, and made cakes in his

21

sight, and did bake the cakes. And she took a pan, and poured them out before him; but he refused to eat. And Amnon said, Have out all men from me. And they went out every man from him. And Amnon said unto Tamar, Bring the meat into the chamber, that I may eat of thine hand. And Tamar took the cakes which she had made, and brought them into the chamber to Amnon her brother".2Sam13:6-10.

- **They don't listen to the voice of reasoning and reality**

"And when she had brought them unto him to eat, he took hold of her, and said unto her, Come lie with me, my sister. And she answered him, Nay, my brother, do not force me; for no such thing ought to be done in Israel: do not thou this folly. And I, whither shall I cause my shame to go? and as for thee, thou shalt be as one of the fools in Israel. Now therefore, I pray thee, speak unto the king; for he will not withhold me from thee. Howbeit he would not hearken unto her voice: but, being stronger than she, forced her, and lay with her"2Sam13:11-14

- **To them love is a feeling and not responsibility**

"Then Amnon hated her exceedingly; so that the hatred wherewith he hated her was greater than the love wherewith he had loved her. And Amnon said unto her, Arise, be gone. And she said unto him, there is no cause: this evil in sending me away is greater than the other that thou didst unto me. But he would not hearken unto her. Then he called his servant that ministered unto him, and said, put now this woman out from me, and bolt the door after her. And she had a garment of divers colours upon her: for with such robes were the king's daughters that were virgins appareled. Then his servant brought her out, and bolted the door after her".2Sam13:15-18.

- It leads to a destructive end where one or both partners usually get burnt and end up crying

"And Tamar put ashes on her head, and rent her garment of divers colours that was on her, and laid her hand on her head, and went on crying. And Absalom her brother said unto her, Hath Amnon thy brother been with thee? but hold now thy peace, my sister: he is thy brother; regard not this thing. So Tamar remained desolate in her brother Absalom's house" 2 Sam. 13:19-20

More True-Life Stories:

- I heard a story whereby a lady repeatedly had abortion for a man because she claimed she loved him and the man loved her. He would repeatedly cry that he loved her, and told her the reason why abortion was good for them and that if the lady loved him then she should consent. Like the other men with this trait, he eventually left her to marry another lady. How can someone claim that having an abortion for him is your prove of love to him? Why should a lady go through the terrible pains of abortion to prove to a self-centered and selfish man that she loves him and thereafter the poor lady is jilted by the same man and left in agony, pains and tears for the rest of her life?
- Another lady asked me a question: I have been dating Wale who I really love for many years and he had a child while in school. I have never seen that as a problem, I have been pregnant for him several times, had many abortions just because he did not want to have another child outside wedlock. Now I have hormonal failure and I'm afraid my chances of carrying another pregnancy is becoming slimmer what should I do? My response was, the lover boy did not want another child outside wedlock and yet he was having sex with you that he claimed to be in love with, without legalizing the union.
- This is another narration told by Mr. Folly:
"I have been in this relationship for some years. I love this lady, but recently she developed a strange attitude that broke my heart.

It started when I had to travel to Lagos, Nigeria, in May. Though we both lived in Ibadan, her school was in Abeokuta, Ogun State, Nigeria. She stopped calling and I was always calling her, her excuse was school work and stress. She even complained of lack of call credit and I would usually send call credit to her line. She came to me and asked me to forgive her, her sin? She met a guy through one of her friends and she was forced to date him. I was hurt but I forgave her, when she got back to school, I didn't observe any change and I decided to visit. She was very cold to me and I knew her heart was with someone else. I kept off and she accused me of being unfaithful. She told me she was home, I went there, didn't see her and when I called, she said she was in school and wanted to try my patience. She visited me, told me she was going home and when I called her in the evening, I heard some voices in the background. She told me they were her brother's friends. I called one of her brothers at home and he said she had left for school and would come home that weekend! She didn't reply my text message when I told her what happened. After a week, she replied and said her brother lied. Should I forget this relationship? I love this girl and would not want to lose her."

I asked the guy, "Could this be love?" If he claims he loves a girl that lies, double dates, sleeps around, pretends and puts him on hold, only to come back from her lustful adventures with the remote control of the heart of the guy in her hand, turning it on and off at will, I am afraid something must be wrong somewhere.

- 'I am a single mother with a kid' said Ms. Luke, 'and I just met a man, who is married and has three kids. He did not live with them because he said his wife was giving him problems. He is now in love with me and I love him also. The problem now is that he still goes to his wife's apartment and he sleeps over there. Whenever I ask him about his whereabouts, his reply would be that he slept there because of his children but he does not love his wife. He is not divorced but he wants to make me his second wife. What should I do? He is ready to take care of me.' Where is the love? Is it with the woman that wants to scatter another

24

woman's home or the man using her for his pleasure and lying that he is keeping his home because of his children?

- Hank had dated Joke for over 10 years starting from their days in the University. They continued while both of them got good jobs. He did not propose marriage neither did he give Joke an opportunity to develop another relationship because he was always all over her. After some years, Joke was forced by circumstances to marry Riley, a former colleague she had known in her university days, who was still as honest as ever but did not sweep her off her feet like Hank. Riley was also not sweet-tongued. Some months after the wedding, Hank called and asked Joke if she would have married him had he proposed earlier? What a question! After how many years? Yet he dated several others after and he is yet to settle down.

- Mary and Chris have been dating for almost eight years and Chris is yet to propose marriage, Mary has a good job so she gives him her salary at the end of the month and the opportunity to travel abroad which her job affords her. However anytime they go out together, he referred to her as his friend because he believed he was not rich enough to marry. He regularly had sex with her, collected her money, and ate the food she prepared with her money. She washed his clothes and took care of all his essentials. Anytime he felt threatened in the relationship, he beat her black and blue. Mary was still clinging to the relationship because she "<u>LOVED</u>" him and he "<u>LOVED</u>" her.

- A lady came to me for advice, she said and I quote,
'I'm in love with him; he's married and I know it's wrong, but I can't help it'.
My response to her was,
"Actually, you can. You can spend an hour listening to stories of women who lost their husbands to infidelity, look into the eyes of their children, hear the betrayal, and see the broken promise in their eyes. When you do, you'll have a re-think."

The biblical and contemporary examples that have been written above should serve as a guide to those who are not in such relationships, not to venture into it. For those who are in it, move out of it fast before your situation becomes unsalvageable. Everyone mentioned in the examples claim to be in love even though none of these examples has an element of true love. The examples all mirror infatuation and lust. Avoid any relationship that drains you and leaves you asking, "How did I get into this?"

If your keeping somebody happy means short-changing the purposes of God for your life and losing your joy, you have overdrawn the budget. When somebody needs too many phone calls, dinners, loans, or other forms of attention, it's time to draw a line simply because such a relationship cannot lead you anywhere; it is nothing but an unhealthy relationship which all of the times lead to pains and tears.

Chapter 3

Relationship That Help in The Fulfillment of Destiny
"Don't Joke with Them"

No one will fulfill divine destiny without the right relationships. Right relationships make the journey to success easier, smoother and faster. On our journey of success, some people move ahead of us while we follow. Other individuals are like guard rails, putting us back on track when we move to the wrong side, away from the road of success; some people also stay behind us to act as support. Others appear suddenly, to do what they have to do in our lives for us to succeed and then they move on their own journey in life. David needed a right relationship in Saul's young daughter, to be saved from an assassination plot by her father. No one can become what God has called him to be without the right relationships. Right relationship helps by supporting us through hard times and acting as a buffer to lessen the burden of personal challenges. If you have a destiny to fulfill without the right relationships around you, the dragon will bring you under a spiritual siege and cut your life short like he did to Samson. Samson was executed because of a wrong relationship that was against the fulfillment of his destiny.

Biblical and Contemporary Examples

Ruth and Naomi

"Now it came to pass in the days when the judges ruled, that there was a famine in the land. And a certain man of Bethlehemjudah went to sojourn in the country of Moab, he, and his wife, and his two sons. And the name of the man was Elimelech, and the name of his wife Naomi, and the name of his two sons Mahlon and Chilion, Ephrathites of Bethlehemjudah. And they came into the country of Moab, and continued there.

And Elimelech Naomi's husband died; and she was left, and her two sons.

And they took them wives of the women of Moab; the name of the one was Orpah, and the name of the other Ruth: and they dwelled there about ten years.

And Mahlon and Chilion died also both of them; and the woman was left of her two sons and her husband.

Then she arose with her daughters-in-law, that she might return from the country of Moab: for she had heard in the country of Moab how that the LORD had visited his people in giving them bread.

Wherefore she went forth out of the place where she was, and her two daughters in law with her; and they went on the way to return unto the land of Judah.

And Naomi said unto her two daughters in law, Go, return each to her mother's house: the LORD deal kindly with you, as ye have dealt with the dead, and with me.

The LORD grant you that ye may find rest, each of you in the house of her husband. Then she kissed them; and they lifted up their voice, and wept.

And they said unto her, Surely, we will return with thee unto thy people.

And Naomi said, turn again, my daughters: why will ye go with me? are there yet any more sons in my womb, that they may be your husbands?

Turn again, my daughters, go your way; for I am too old to have an husband. If I should say, I have hope, if I should have an husband also tonight, and should also bear sons;

Would ye tarry for them till they were grown? would ye stay for them from having husbands? nay, my daughters; for it grieveth me much for your sakes that the hand of the LORD is gone out against me.

And they lifted up their voice, and wept again: and Orpah kissed her mother in law; but Ruth clave unto her.

And she said, Behold, thy sister in law is gone back unto her people, and unto her gods: return thou after thy sister in law.

And Ruth said, Intreat me not to leave thee, or to return from following after thee: for whither thou goest, I will go; and where thou lodgest, I will lodge: thy people shall be my people, and thy God my God:

Where thou diest, will I die, and there will I be buried: the LORD do so to me, and more also, if ought but death part thee and me." Ruth 1: 1-17. [Emphasis added.]

Naomi was a mother-in-law to Ruth who was a Moabite, whose culture and god was different from the God of Israel. After Naomi lost her husband and sons, she decided to return to Judah, so she asked her daughters-in-law to return to their people and country but Ruth totally refused to return. This type of relationship can exist between the same sex or opposite sex, individual just wants to stay with you in your period of pain, or when you need help. These individuals just appear on board your journey of success ready to go all the way with you. They are not fair-weather friends; they stay with you at the crossroads of life when you have lost a sense of direction and purpose. They believe in you even when you do not believe in yourself.

"And Naomi said, turn again, my daughters: why will ye go with me? are there yet any more sons in my womb, that they may be your husbands?
Turn again, my daughters, go your way; for I am too old to have an husband. If I should say, I have hope, if I should have an husband also to night, and should also bear sons;
Would ye tarry for them till they were grown? would ye stay for them from having husbands? nay, my daughters; for it grieveth me much for your sakes that the hand of the LORD is gone out against me Ruth"
1: 11 – 13

"And Ruth said, intreat me not to leave thee, or to return from following after thee; for whither thou goest, I will go; and where thou lodgest, I will lodge; thy people shall be my people and thy/god my God. Ruth 1: 16.

Ruth stuck to her mother – in – law even in the face of hardship, poverty and uncertainties.

"And Ruth, the Moabites said unto Naomi, let me now go to the field, and glean ears of corn after him in whose sight I shall find grace. And she said unto her, go my daughter." Ruth 2:2.

Sometimes this type of relationship exists between opposite sex but it does not mean that the relationship will lead to marriage. It can also exist between a senior and a junior either in school or at the place of work.

- When I was in secondary school, Mrs. Hope was one of the best English teachers in my school. One day she came into a class of combined students studying Arts and Science subjects. She asked for the meaning of an English word and I was the only student that knew the answer. She was surprised because I was a science student. The teacher was so impressed that she promised to prepare me for free for my secondary school leaving external examination. She stood by her words and by the time the result of the West African School Certificate examination was out, I was one of the few lucky students that passed English language just because she took me through the fundamentals, giving me tons of questions, at the same time marking them all. At the beginning, my scores were low because she was using the external examination standard to mark my scripts, after each session with her, my mark kept increasing, She pushed and encouraged me and after I consistently got a particular grade she was pleased with, she finally released me saying she was very sure and confident that I would have at least a credit pass.

"And Boaz answered and said unto her, it hath fully been shewed me all that thou hast done unto thy mother – in – law since the death of thine husband and how thou hast left thy father and thy mother, and the land of thy nativity and art come unto a people which thou knowest not heretofore". Ruth 2:11.

"So she kept fast by the maidens of Boaz to glean unto the end of barley harvest and of wheat harvest and dwelt with her mother – in – law. Ruth 2:23.

Ruth was indeed a divine helper to Naomi. In the part of Africa where I come from Naomi would have suffered and died of frustration before her time, because she would naturally be addressed as a witch, stigmatized that she killed her husband and two sons in a foreign land and returned unhurt even though she was hurt emotionally, which is of less importance to them. She would eventually be ostracized to the extent that no child will be allowed to run errands for her because of the fear that she would kill them, since she had no child of her own. No woman will allow her husband to come near her in this circumstance; the women will stare at her and frustrate her with their tongues. She would have died a frustrated and miserable old woman, if not for her divine helper who followed her through the hills, desert and mountains into the land of Israel. Naomi stayed indoor to save herself of stares and shame while the young woman Ruth, went to scout around for grains of wheat and barley for food to save herself and her mother-in-law (who could not move around freely) from hunger. She was indeed a divine helper and her behaviour eventually brought friendship and honour to the life of Naomi.

"And the women said unto Naomi, blessed be the LORD, which hath not left thee this day without a kinsman, that his name may be famous in Israel.
And he shall be unto thee a restorer of thy life, and a nourisher of thine old age: for thy daughter in law, which loveth thee, which is better to thee than seven sons, hath born him." Ruth 4: 14-15.

So where Naomi was not supposed to raise her head or voice she became a celebrity because of her divine helper. And the latter end of Naomi was much more beautiful than her beginning.
"And Naomi took the child, and laid it in her bosom, and became nurse unto it.
And the women her neighbours gave it a name, saying, there is a son born to Naomi; and they called his name Obed: he is the father of Jesse, the father of David. Ruth 4: 16 – 17"

Obed eventually became the great grandfather of Jesus.
"So Boaz took Ruth, and she was his wife: and when he went in unto her, the LORD gave her conception, and she bare a son.

And the women her neighbours gave it a name, saying, there is a son born to Naomi; and they called his name Obed: he is the father of Jesse, the father of David." Ruth 4: 13& 17.

The Paralytic Man and His Friends

"And, behold, men brought in a bed a man which was taken with a palsy: and they sought means to bring him in, and to lay him before him.
And when they could not find by what way they might bring him in because of the multitude, they went upon the housetop, and let him down through the tiling with his couch into the midst before Jesus." Luke 5: 18 – 19.

The man in the story above was sick and paralytic, which means he could not walk nor work because he was paralyzed. Paralysis had sentenced him to lying down on the bed for the rest of his life. He ate, urinated and defecated in one spot. Even if he had a very strong desire to see Jesus, he could not get there because of his condition. He needed people to take him to the healer and a day came, God connected him to his divine helpers because they decided that no matter the cost and sacrifice it would take them, they would make sure the paralytic man saw Jesus. Note that, the helpers might not have money to give him which might be what he felt he needed most. They might never have brought him food for once. Some of them may not be able to help pack his excreta, because they got easily nauseated but they were all strong and determined enough to break the roof of a house for them to let him down at the feet of Jesus. We meet different people for different reasons in our journey through life. We must identify the reason(s) why they journeyed with us, so that we do not ultimately miss the blessing of that relationship.

"But that ye may know that the Son of man hath power upon earth to forgive sins, (he said unto the sick of the palsy,) I say unto thee, Arise, and take up thy couch, and go into thine house.
And immediately he rose up before them, and took up that whereon he lay, and departed to his own house, glorifying God." Luke 5: 24 – 25

The man got back the use of his legs, because of the strong determination and doggedness of his divine helpers. If he had not been helped, he might have remained paralytic forever.

- "George Washington Carver spent his early years shuffled between foster homes, until Maria Watkins, a washer woman, found him asleep in her barn. She took him in, and then took him to church where he introduced Jesus to him. When he eventually left her home, he took with him the Bible she had given him. Maria left her mark on his life and George left his mark on the world. This father of modern agriculture was a friend to three presidents as well as Henry Ford and Gandhi. He is credited with over three hundred different inventions.

- Eleven years ago, I went to minister in a church and Mrs Sasere of Mount Zion Faith Ministry International was also invited to the programme. After the ministrations, we got talking and she invited me to a couple's programme organized by the Mount Zion Faith Ministries International Crew in Ibadan, Oyo State, Nigeria. I went to the programme with my husband. At the programme, we were opportune to meet Pastor Bisi Adewale [An international preacher and an author of several books]. A year after we also invited Pastor Bisi Adewale to a programme we organized in my own church. During one of the breaks we got talking in the office and he stumbled on a message I preached at a programme that was printed in a booklet. After reading through, he made one or two corrections and said "Your generation and generations yet unborn will not forgive you if you don't write a book."

Although I am a voracious reader but I don't know anything about publishing a book, but I took up the challenge. During the course of my gathering up materials for my first book, *Keys to a Fulfilling Marriage.*" I stumbled on a jotter that I used for writing messages in my University days. While going through it,

33

I saw that I wrote inside that jotter about ten years before then that "one day I am going to write a book."

Also, during this period, the publisher of my first book Pastor (Mrs.) Olajumoke Adedamola came my way. She needed a favour and someone told her I could be of help to her. She later gave me a copy of her very beautiful book and I was surprised that it was achieved by someone I was meeting, so I told her about my dream of writing. She was the one who started putting the final icing on the cake to achieve *"Keys to a Fulfilling Marriage"*.

Bath-sheba and Prophet Nathan

Bathsheba, a beautiful woman, was having her bath after days of menstruating. She was purifying herself according to the Jewish custom and the law of Moses which had made her to be separated for some time. She was celebrating the bath of freedom to mingle again, from the loneliness of being ostracized. Coupled with the fact that her husband was at the warfront, she was having her bath in her own compound. Unknown to her that the king's tall palace overlooked her own bathroom. She finished bathing and was probably dressing up to visit her grandfather Ahitophel to ask about her husband when she heard a knock. On opening the door, she saw the king's messenger who told her the king wanted to see her immediately. The king was no other person than the chosen of God, King David. Perhaps, she was thinking within her maybe the king could have words from her husband. When she got to the king and he made the most unholy request, who was she to reject?

"And it came to pass in an evening tide, that David arose from off his bed, and walked upon the roof of the king's house: and from the roof he saw a woman washing herself; and the woman was very beautiful to look upon.
And David sent and enquired after the woman. And one said, Is not this Bath-sheba, the daughter of Eliam, the wife of Uriah the Hittite?
And David sent messengers, and took her; and she came in unto him, and he lay with her; for she was purified from her uncleanness: and she returned unto her house." 2 Sam. 11: 2 – 4.

34

Bath-sheba got pregnant after the encounter with the king. She sent words to King David that she was carrying his child.

"And the woman conceived, and sent and told David, and said, I am with child." 2 Sam 11:5.

Unknown to her the king was trying to cover his sin. So, in the process her husband the patriotic soldier of Israel had to die.

And he wrote in the letter, saying, set ye Uriah in the forefront of the hottest battle, and retire ye from him, that he may be smitten, and die.
And it came to pass, when Joab observed the city, that he assigned Uriah unto a place where he knew that valiant men were.
And the men of the city went out, and fought with Joab: and there fell some of the people of the servants of David; and Uriah the Hittite died also." 2 Sam. 11:15–17.

King David married Bathsheba after the death and mourning of her husband. Probably, after a month her tummy was already protruding like a three months old pregnancy and before long, tongues started wagging on how she committed adultery with the king and killed her own husband to cover up. The whole city heard different versions of what happened, so different opinions were formed about her. Suddenly God came on the scene through the great Prophet Nathan to confront King David with his sins.

"And the LORD sent Nathan unto David. And he came unto him, and said unto him, there were two men in one city; the one rich, and the other poor.
Wherefore hast thou despised the commandment of the LORD, to do evil in his sight? thou hast killed Uriah the Hittite with the sword, and hast taken his wife to be thy wife, and hast slain him with the sword of the children of Ammon.
For thou didst it secretly: but I will do this thing before all Israel, and before the sun." 2 Sam 12:1, 9 & 12.

Everybody in the palace including Bathsheba must have been worried about the presence of Prophet Nathan. May be David confided in Bathsheba, which would have made her know that Prophet Nathan and God were probably against her too. The baby died shortly after he was born, because he was also not spared by God.

"Howbeit, because by this deed thou hast given great occasion to the enemies of the LORD to blaspheme, the child also that is born unto thee shall surely die.
And Nathan departed unto his house. And the LORD struck the child that Uriah's wife bare unto David, and it was very sick.
David therefore besought God for the child; and David fasted, and went in, and lay all night upon the earth.
And the elders of his house arose, and went to him, to raise him up from the earth: but he would not, neither did he eat bread with them.
And it came to pass on the seventh day, that the child died. And the servants of David feared to tell him that the child was dead: for they said, Behold, while the child was yet alive, we spake unto him, and he would not hearken unto our voice: how will he then vex himself, if we tell him that the child is dead?
But when David saw that his servants whispered, David perceived that the child was dead: therefore David said unto his servants, Is the child dead? And they said, He is dead.
Then David arose from the earth, and washed, and anointed himself, and changed his apparel, and came into the house of the LORD, and worshipped: then he came to his own house; and when he required, they set bread before him, and he did eat.
Then said his servants unto him, What thing is this that thou hast done? thou didst fast and weep for the child, while it was alive; but when the child was dead, thou didst rise and eat bread.
And he said, While the child was yet alive, I fasted and wept: for I said, who can tell whether GOD will be gracious to me, that the child may live? But now he is dead, wherefore should I fast? can I bring him back again? I shall go to him, but he shall not return to me.
And David comforted Bath-sheba his wife, and went in unto her, and lay with her: and she bare a son, and he called his name Solomon: and the LORD loved him." 2 Sam. 12:14-23.

36

The same Prophet Nathan that gave God's verdict and judgment because of the sin David committed disappeared from the palace, only to re-appear later in another book of the Bible as a friend, mentor, guide, and divine helper and greatest of all, an ally to Bathsheba in the fulfillment of David's promise to Bathsheba concerning her son, Solomon.

"Wherefore Nathan spake unto Bath-sheba the mother of Solomon, saying, Hast thou not heard that Adonijah the son of Haggith doth reign, and David our lord knoweth it not?
Now therefore come, let me, I pray thee, give thee counsel, that thou mayest save thine own life, and the life of thy son Solomon.
Go and get thee in unto king David, and say unto him, Didst not thou, my lord, O king, swear unto thine handmaid, saying, Assuredly Solomon thy son shall reign after me, and he shall sit upon my throne? why then doth Adonijah reign?
Behold, while thou yet talkest there with the king, I also will come in after thee, and confirm thy words."1 Kings 1: 11 -14.

"And, lo, while she yet talked with the king, Nathan the prophet also came in.
And they told the king, saying, Behold Nathan the prophet. And when he was come in before the king, he bowed himself before the king with his face to the ground.
And Nathan said, My lord, O king, hast thou said, Adonijah shall reign after me, and he shall sit upon my throne?"
"And king David said, Call me Zadok the priest, and Nathan the prophet, and Benaiah the son of Jehoiada. And they came before the king.
The king also said unto them, take with you the servants of your lord, and cause Solomon my son to ride upon mine own mule, and bring him down to Gihon:
And let Zadok the priest and Nathan the prophet anoint him there king over Israel: and blow ye with the trumpet, and say, God save king Solomon.

Then ye shall come up after him, that he may come and sit upon my throne; for he shall be king in my stead: and I have appointed him to be ruler over Israel and over Judah.

And Benaiah the son of Jehoiada answered the king, and said, Amen: the LORD God of my lord the king say so too.

As the LORD hath been with my lord the king, even so be he with Solomon, and make his throne greater than the throne of my lord king David.

So Zadok the priest, and Nathan the prophet, and Benaiah the son of Jehoiada, and the Cherethites, and the Pelethites, went down, and caused Solomon to ride upon king David's mule, and brought him to Gihon.

And Zadok the priest took an horn of oil out of the tabernacle, and anointed Solomon. And they blew the trumpet; and all the people said, God save King Solomon."1 Kings 1: 22 – 24, 32 – 39.

Through his divine help, Solomon, Bathsheba's son became the king of Israel even though Solomon was not the first born of David, but David had made an earlier promise to Bathsheba. Adonijah, one of David's sons conspired with some members of David's cabinet to take over the throne, because David was already an old man. The same Prophet Nathan was the one that told Bathsheba about it. He also stood by Bathsheba through the period of struggle for the throne.

In the course of your journey in life, you meet this type of people either by accident or just finding them along your path and they give you direction, follow, nudge, encourage, appreciate, or scold you. They often see something in you that you never saw and they follow you till you get to a safe harbor in life. Solomon the son of Bathsheba became the wisest and richest king that ever lived.

CHAPTER 4

Relationships That Are Stable All Year Round
"If You Are In It, Value It"

According to *Oxford Learner's dictionary,* the word "stable" means; resistant to change of position or condition, firm and dependable; subject to little fluctuation, and maintaining equilibrium. Therefore, a stable relationship is where one of the partners involved is resistant and unaffected by the unloving act usually exhibited by the other partner. They are usually forced on the other person by different circumstances. Some of the couples in this type of relationship find love along the way, while some don't. The seemingly disadvantaged partner does not usually have anything striking in their outward appearance; the strength of character is usually their advantage. The spouse that is not loved most times doesn't threaten the existence of the relationship, loyalty is their drive, no matter what the erring partner does the spouse is always waiting with open arms, begging to be loved or appreciating the little love that is given, they are like a dry sponge that soaks up every little water dropped on it. Most times because one of them just stays in the relationship and is not ready to leave, the relationship usually lasts till death do them part.

Sometimes, emotional pull is with one to the other and at times it just does not exist between both of them, but because they respect vows, they both stay committed and loyal to the bond. In such relationships, there are no hot or cold periods of expression of love.

Biblical and Contemporary Examples
Leah and Jacob

"Leah had weak eyes, but Rachel was lovely in form and beautiful"
Gen. 29:17 {NIV}

Leah the first wife of Jacob is just like your regular next-door girl, who does not have a striking, beauty; only on closer look do you see that she is not really ugly. However, she is homely, unassuming and just herself anytime you see her. In this type of relationship, you see a type of Leah as someone who craves for love but does not talk or push you to love her. You can always trust that such people will not let you down, will not betray trust but keep to the covenant no matter what you do to them. They have this stubborn streak in them that makes them to hold on in spite of the opposition around them.

"And when the LORD saw that Leah was hated, he opened her womb: but Rachel was barren." Gen. 29:31

God also had pity on Leah, so He opened her womb because she was unloved for no just reason, but may be for flimsy excuses such as 'she is not captivating, smashing, dazzling, head turning, mouth dropping, and glaringly beautiful'. So, God opened her womb to provide a home for her and the husband. In most cases such men or women do not appreciate their spouses; they are usually taken for granted. Most people in this type of relationship were forced on each other because the parent of one spouse wanted the marriage, like Jacob was deceitfully forced to marry Leah, due to tradition where the younger must not marry before the elder. At other times it is because pregnancy occurred and they have to compulsorily marry each other.

"When morning came, there was Leah! So Jacob said to Laban, "what is this you have done to me? I served you for Rachael, didn't I? Why have you deceived me?" Laban replied "it is not our custom here, to give the younger daughter in marriage before the older one, finish this daughter's bridal week: then we will give you the younger one also, in return for another seven years of work." Gen. 29:25-27

Jacob got married to Leah by circumstances beyond his control.

*"And Leah conceived, and bare a son, and she called his name
Reuben: for she said, Surely the LORD hath looked upon my
affliction; now therefore my husband will love me.*
*And she conceived again, and bare a son; and said, Because the LORD
hath heard that I was hated, he hath therefore given me this son also:
and she called his name Simeon.*
*And she conceived again, and bare a son; and said, now this time will
my husband be joined unto me, because I have born him three sons:
therefore was his name called Levi.*
*And she conceived again, and bare a son: and she said, now will I
praise the LORD: therefore, she called his name Judah; and left
bearing." Gen. 29: 32 – 35[Emphasis added]*

Her thirst for her husband's love could be felt even in the names she gave
to her children. Her firstborn's name "Reuben" means "surely the LORD
hath looked upon my affliction, now therefore my husband will love
me". The second "Simeon" she said "Because the LORD hath heard that
I was hated", the third "Levi" she said "Now this time, will my husband
be joined unto me".

At this point, I want to tell the bachelors and spinsters reading this book
that you must never marry someone you don't love or who does not love
you because if you do, they will make life miserable, uneventful and
torturous for you. Leah felt she could buy the love of her husband
because of the children, but it never worked that way. I remember an
adage from my tribe that says. "A woman whom a man loves, loves her
children". Don't marry someone you are not proud of.

The singles should also not base their relationships only on what they
can see like beauty, colour, stature, height etc. These are outwards things
that are important but not the most important, and always remember that
not all that glitters is gold. Sometimes, that person that you think is plain
might actually be the will of God for you in marriage. Therefore, before
you make your next move into marriage, make sure you pray and pray
well. God can never make mistakes if you let Him lead and direct you.

Marrying someone you don't love will lead to bitterness.

"And she said unto her, is it a small matter that thou hast even taken my husband? And wouldest thou take away my son's mandrakes".

Leah was bitter that her husband did not love her and was not giving her attention even after all the children she had for him. This could be deduced from the tone of her response to Rachel after she asked for some mandrakes from Leah's son. After four sons from Leah and one from her handmaid; Leah still had to buy the love and attention of her husband for a night from her sister, Rachel, in exchange for Reuben's mandrakes.

Where God's hand is, there His blessings will be, so before you go into that relationship make sure you get a go ahead from God. In case you are already married either by your choice or the choice of others like in the case of Leah, and you feel you don't love the person that much, remember that love can still be given a chance to grow. Check your reasons for not loving the person, work on the ones you can work on but more importantly, you have to face reality of what you have on ground. Remember that a bird in hand is worth two in the bush. So listen to the voice of reality. It is not about today but tomorrow. The guy or lady you are 'managing' in a relationship or that lady you feel is not your 'class' could as well be the key to your destiny. I also discovered that some of the excuses given for not loving this particular spouse include: "He or she is not well educated", "does not know how to speak good English, dress well, receive visitors, has tribal marks, too short or too tall, too light in complexion or too dark" etc. Please don't abandon that stable relationship for lust or infatuation because, if you look very well, you will discover very good innate qualities in him or her and where there is a will there will definitely be a way.

Ruth and Boaz

In the case of Ruth, her mother- in - law felt Ruth could be married to Boaz. According to their custom, Boaz being a close relation of Naomi's late husband could marry her and inherit all that belong to the deceased. In turn, he would raise up a child in the name of the deceased. The basis for the relationship therefore, was not love, compatibility or hearing from God. They had met one or two times while she was gleaning wheat after his reapers on his farm. There might have been few occasions when they exchanged pleasantries, which of course will be few because of the difference in status. She was a widow and he a rich single man who was probably much older because he referred to her as his daughter. The way Boaz saw Ruth was probably that of a mere kinsman, so he saw the young and the older widow as his responsibility.

"Then said Boaz unto Ruth, hearest thou not, my daughter? Go not to glean in another field, neither go from hence, but abide here fast by my maidens:
Let thine eyes be on the field that they do reap, and go thou after them: have I not charged the young men that they shall not touch thee? and when thou art athirst, go unto the vessels, and drink of that which the young men have drawn." Ruth 2: 8 – 9

So, on one of the few occasions they met, he asked her to glean only in his field and gave her permission to drink water. It was more like showing respect and being kind to Naomi because of Ruth's loyalty to the family.

"And now is not Boaz of our kindred, with whose maidens thou wast? Behold, he winnoweth barley to night in the threshing floor.
Wash thyself therefore, and anoint thee, and put thy raiment upon thee, and get thee down to the floor: but make not thyself known unto the man, until he shall have done eating and drinking.
And it shall be, when he lieth down, that thou shalt mark the place where he shall lie, and thou shalt go in, and uncover his feet, and lay thee down; and he will tell thee what thou shalt do.
And she said unto her, all that thou sayest unto me I will do.
And she went down unto the floor, and did according to all that her mother in law bade her.
And when Boaz had eaten and drunk, and his heart was merry, he went to lie down at the end of the heap of corn: and she came softly, and uncovered his feet, and laid her down.
And it came to pass at midnight, that the man was afraid, and turned himself: and, behold, a woman lay at his feet.
And he said, Who art thou? And she answered, I am Ruth thine handmaid: spread therefore thy skirt over thine handmaid; for thou art a near kinsman.

And he said, blessed be thou of the LORD, my daughter: for thou hast shewed more kindness in the latter end than at the beginning, inasmuch as thou followedst not young men, whether poor or rich.

And now, my daughter, fear not; I will do to thee all that thou requirest: for all the city of my people doth know that thou art a virtuous woman.

And now it is true that I am thy near kinsman: howbeit there is a kinsman nearer than I.

Tarry this night, and it shall be in the morning, that if he will perform unto thee the part of a kinsman, well; let him do the kinsman's part: but if he will not do the part of a kinsman to thee, then will I do the part of a kinsman to thee, as the LORD liveth: lie down until the morning.

And she lay at his feet until the morning: and she rose up before one could know another. And he said, let it not be known that a woman came into the floor.

Also he said, Bring the vail that thou hast upon thee, and hold it. And when she held it, he measured six measures of barley, and laid it on her: and she went into the city." Ruth 3:2 – 15

"Moreover Ruth the Moabitess, the wife of Mahlon, have I purchased to be my wife, to raise up the name of the dead upon his inheritance, that the name of the dead be not cut off from among his brethren, and from the gate of his place: ye are witnesses this day.

And all the people that were in the gate, and the elders, said, we are witnesses. The LORD make the woman that is come into thine house like Rachel and like Leah, which two did build the house of Israel: and do thou worthily in Ephrathah, and be famous in Bethlehem:

And let thy house be like the house of Pharez, whom Tamar bare unto Judah, of the seed which the LORD shall give thee of this young woman.

So Boaz took Ruth, and she was his wife: and when he went in unto her, the LORD gave her conception, and she bare a son." Ruth 4: 10 – 13

Obligations and commitments is usually the first reason for the existence of this type of relationship.

Boaz, a shy but matured man living among his people, and Ruth a young widow, living in a strange land with little or no choice left. They were both arranged to meet each other by Mama Naomi, so they got married by obligation to a widowed mother- in- law and to a dead relation.

Jacob was young and handsome so he had a choice of whom to marry but in Leah's case she was getting old, at least compared to her age mates and even younger ones that had married or already had suitors. Nobody was asking for her hand in marriage. Leah's father arranged for her to be married to a man who had seen her but had made his choice in another woman whom he loved very dearly. To Jacob therefore, Leah did not exist in that home and just may-be she loved Jacob and she had made several attempts for him to notice her but it never worked. She also accepted the father's plan, thinking Jacob will love her, after seeing her good qualities but it never happened. Jacob stayed in the relationship, after he had slept with her and the father-in-law have consented to still give him his heartthrob, so he stayed in the relationship out of obligation.

> *"Leah was tender eyed; but Rachel was beautiful and well-favoured.*
> *And Jacob loved Rachel; and said, I will serve thee seven years for Rachel thy younger daughter.*
> *And Laban said, it is better that I give her to thee, than that I should give her to another man: abide with me.*
> *And Jacob served seven years for Rachel; and they seemed unto him but a few days, for the love he had to her.*
> *And Jacob said unto Laban, give me my wife, for my days are fulfilled, that I may go in unto her." Gen. 29:17 – 21*

Those that are matured enough find love or give love a chance to grow. In the relationship that existed between Ruth and Boaz, love was not mentioned but of course love is important in any relationship. However, for one reason or the other some relationships have to start without it. In the days of our parents, some people were married off even before they knew their left from their right or in cases where two matured singles were introduced to each other and they got married by proxy.

- Mrs. Dave loved her handsome husband who was always out with other ladies. She awaited him dutifully, was never ruffled with his behaviour and like a dry sponge she soaked in any little love that was left in the man for her. When I met her while in secondary school, as a young girl I felt it was wrong for her to speak highly of her husband. I also felt the man did not deserve a woman like her. She was not astonishingly beautiful but she was a beautiful woman on the inside. She kept the home running smoothly; took care of the children, her business and all the man's needs but she in turn was not shown love by the husband because he was forced to marry her.

- A cousin of mine was working in the city, when the family felt he was not getting younger and there was no sign of a woman in the horizon. His mum and sisters promptly found a girl from the village for him. The mum claimed that she and the girl's mum were neighbors in the market (where they sold vegetables) and she had seen how enterprising the lady could be. My cousin kicked against the arrangement. He was used to city girls but could not 'net' any of them in marriage and grudgingly settled for the girl that his mum recommended.

As soon as the girl joined him in the city, she began to cook a few cups of jollof rice to sell in the front of their house- once the husband left for work. He only knew what hit him when people began coming to the house to place orders for her food. Her efforts to help financially were always embarrassing to him but she was not used to staying idle. Later on, she began to sell flour for bakeries.

In less than a year, after their marriage, her husband was retrenched at work with a severance pay due to economic meltdown which led to downsizing in his place of work. Following her advice (he was not the entrepreneurial type) he invested into the business. Today, they are major distributors of flour to a prominent brand. They have cars, and houses in the city as well as in the village and blessed with, two girls and a boy. The same lady sends a certain amount of money to her mother-in-law on monthly basis for her upkeep. Something, her son was not doing.... besides giving her money whenever he visited home.

• A lawyer friend told me a story of a man and his wife who were in the middle of a bitter divorce when it was suddenly discovered that the woman had cancer of the breast. The man that she had almost divorced wasted no time in rushing to her side with his money and moral support to face the medical battle with her. When asked why he did what he did considering their ongoing bitter divorce, he told all that cared to listen that it would be very mean of him if he watched that woman die without lifting a finger to assist. He said that even though they have grown apart he still would not forget the 'wonderful' wife of his youth that was so good to him, when things had not fallen apart in their marriage.

CHAPTER 5

Mentor-Friend Relationship
"Ladder to Go Up"

A mentor is an experienced and trusted counselor or an adviser of an inexperienced person; they are usually older and more experienced. They help to guide an individual's development. A mentor can help a mentee improve his or her abilities and skills through observation, assessment, moulding and by providing guidance. Much like any other relationship a mentor-mentee relationship takes work from both sides. Mentoring is an effective method of helping inexperienced individuals develop and progress in their profession.

Biblical and Contemporary Examples

Eli and Samuel
Eli was a great man of God in the land of Israel,
"Now Eli the priest sat upon a seat by a post of the temple of the LORD." 1 Sam. 1: 9b
Hannah the mother of Samuel was barren for some years after which God answered her and gave her Samuel. In fulfillment of her vow, she returned the boy Samuel to the Lord to be mentored by Prophet Eli.
"And when she had weaned him, she took him up with her, with three bullocks, and one ephah of flour, and a bottle of wine, and brought him unto the house of the LORD in Shiloh: and the child was young.
And they slew a bullock, and brought the child to Eli.
And she said, Oh my lord, as thy soul liveth, my lord, I am the woman that stood by thee here, praying unto the LORD.
For this child I prayed; and the LORD hath given me my petition which I asked of him:

Therefore, also I have lent him to the LORD; as long as he liveth he shall be lent to the LORD. And he worshipped the LORD there". 1 Sam. 1:24-28

Right under the watchful eyes of Prophet Eli, Samuel was taught how to minister to the Lord.

"And Elkanah went to Ramah to his house. And the child did minister unto the LORD before Eli the priest."
"But Samuel ministered before the LORD, being a child, girded with a linen ephod". 1 Sam. 2: 11 and 18

He continued to grow before the Lord and was taught about the sacrifices and rituals of the temple, so much that the people of Israel loved him.

"And the child Samuel grew on, and was in favor both with the LORD, and also with men".1 Sam. 2:26

God called Samuel in an audible voice, but he had not recognized the voice of God and how to answer.
"That the LORD called Samuel: and he answered, here am I.
And he ran unto Eli, and said, here am I; for thou calledst me. And he said I called not; lie down again. And he went and lay down.
And the LORD called yet again, Samuel. And Samuel arose and went to Eli, and said, here am I; for thou didst call me. And he answered, I called not, my son; lie down again.
Now Samuel did not yet know the LORD, neither was the word of the LORD yet revealed unto him". 1Sam3:4-7

Prophet Eli had been in the ministry for quite some time, so he knew some things about God which Samuel was yet to know. Samuel went to him after the third time thinking the great Prophet Eli was calling him. That was when Prophet Eli told him what to do. Samuel was mentored by Prophet Eli on how to recognize the voice of God and respond to it.

"And the LORD called Samuel again the third time. And he arose and went to Eli, and said, here am I; for thou didst call me. And Eli perceived that the LORD had called the child.
Therefore Eli said unto Samuel, Go, lie down: and it shall be, if he call thee, that thou shalt say, Speak, LORD; for thy servant heareth. So Samuel went and lay down in his place.
And the LORD came, and stood, and called as at other times, Samuel, Samuel. Then Samuel answered, Speak; for thy servant heareth." 1 Sam3:8-10

Samuel grew so much to become the greatest and last prophet to rule and judge over the great nation of Israel.

Naomi and Ruth
"And Ruth the Moabitess said unto Naomi, let me now go to the field, and glean ears of corn after him in whose sight I shall find grace. And she said unto her, Go, my daughter." Ruth 2:2

Ruth turned her life around when she was bereaved, broke and barren. How?
First by choosing the right mentor, "…wherever you go, I will go…"
"And Ruth said, Intreat me not to leave thee, or to return from following after thee: for whither thou goest, I will go; and where thou lodgest, I will lodge: thy people shall be my people, and thy God my God." Ruth 1:16
The fact that Naomi was a Jew and Ruth a Gentile, or that Ruth was young and Naomi was older, didn't put Ruth off one bit. Doubtless, there were times they didn't see eye to eye or relate to each other, at all. However, when God wants to stretch you, He will put somebody into your life with different experiences and insight. Naomi was Ruth's eyes and ears in a world she didn't know and her tutor cum guide in getting Ruth to her destiny. God is raising up leaders with solution to today's problems. If you hope to be called for duty, recognize those He sent to prepare you whether they come to cheer, comfort, counsel or correct you.

Secondly, by getting into the right field. Ruth said, "let me glean after him in whose sight I might find favour". Things were bad in Moab, but were good in Bethlehem. Ruth left the comfort of the familiar and stepped out in faith and not only ended up surviving but thriving. In the end she married Boaz, the owner of the field. She went on to become part of the lineage of King David and our Lord Jesus Christ. God's plan for your future, involves connecting you with the right people and being in the right field.

- Aliko Dangote was born into a wealthy home in Kano State, Nigeria. He got his first degree in Cairo Egypt. He had always loved trading. Reports have it that his first trial at entrepreneurship was when he sold sweets to his classmates as a primary school pupil, even though his family was wealthy. His grandfather, Sanusi Dantata became Dangote's guardian in 1965 after the death of his father. Having spent most of his childhood with his grandfather; he quickly became interested in the world of business after graduating from college. Aliko Dangote's journey to fortune is not a rag to riches story because he is from a wealthy family. However, the loan he got from his uncle was the spring board for him. The success story of Aliko Dangote can be traced to his mentor who happened to be his grandfather Sanusi Dantata who was a successful businessman in his time. He gave him a small capital to start his own business and an additional loan of five hundred thousand naira, which was not small money in those days. Dangote was supposed to repay the loan in 4years which was when the business was expected to have begun yielding profits. However, he was able to repay the loan within 6months under the guidance of his mentor from whom he had learned the different rudiments of entrepreneurship; like marketing, procuring goods, establishing customer relationship and more. Aliko was quoted as saying 'Interest, determination, insight, vision, guidance and assistance from my grandfather Sanusi Dantata were what built the empire I have today'. Aliko Dangote is the richest person on the African continent with a net worth of 13.9 billion USD according to Forbes 2018 ranking.
- American business magnate Warren Buffet is often considered the most successful investor of the twentieth century. The Berkshire Hathaway CEO mentored Microsoft co-founder Bill

Gates. Gates first met Buffet at a dinner organized by Gate's mother, where the two spoke about business and philanthropy. Gates admits that over the years he has turned to Buffet for advices on various subjects, and has often referred to Buffet as one of a kind.

- Virgin group co-founder Richard Branson has personally benefited from a mentor- mentee relationship, Branson asked British airline entrepreneur Sir Freddie Laker for guidance during his struggle to get multinational conglomerate Virgin Atlantic off the ground. It is always good to have a helping hand at the start. Branson has been quoted as saying. 'I wouldn't have gotten anywhere in the airline industry without the mentorship of Sir Freddie Lake'.

- Michael Jordan said, "Other than my parents, no one had a bigger influence on my life than Coach Dean Smith. He was more than a coach- he was my mentor, my teacher, my second father. Coach was always there for me whenever I needed him and I loved him for it. Not only in teaching me the game of basketball, he taught me about life too".

- Oprah Winfrey was mentored by celebrated author and poet, the late Maya Angelou., Oprah Winfrey known for her talk show said, "She was there for me always, guiding me through some of the most important years of my life. Behind every successful person, there's a mentor who helped them along the way.
- Former More House College President, Dr. Benjamin Mays was an outspoken critic of segregation before the rise of the modern civil rights movement and a mentor to Dr. Martin Luther King Jr. The two men met during King's undergraduate years at More House College and remained close until king's death in 1968. May's emphasized on two ideas in particular;
  o The dignity of all human beings

- o The compatibility of American democratic ideals with American social practices became vital strains in King's language and in the civil right movement.

- Former super bowl champion, Darrel Green was mentored by his middle school football coach, "I had a coach who in a different way encouraged me that I could be a great running athlete. He was always encouraging me to participate, and I did and so I think he helped me to identify the possibilities, which I never even thought about." Green said.

- Mother Theresa committed her life to helping others and was recognised as one of the most admirable people of the twentieth century. Operating orphanages, AIDS hospices, and other charities worldwide. She led a remarkable and revered life, but may not have achieved all that she did if it weren't for her mentor, Father Michael Van der Peet. The two met while waiting for a bus in Rome and quickly developed a close friendship. They spoke regularly and confided in each other over the years.

- Retired basketball player and board member Bill Russel played center for the Boston Celtics from 1956 to 1969. His mother was his greatest mentor. "My mother taught me to stand up for myself, to use my brain power on my behalf" he said. Russel's mother died when he was twelve, but he continued to live through her guidance. "More strongly than ever, she stayed with me in my thoughts, my goals, my aspirations, her presence; her teachings remained with me when she was not around."

-

Chapter 6

Relationship with God

"The Most Important"

"I am the vine; you are the branches, if a man remains in me and I in him, he will bear much fruit; apart from me you can do nothing".
John 15:5 NKJV

The first and the best relationship anyone can have is with God. The bible gives us two interesting pictures of how our relationship with Jesus should be.

- **A Branch**: I am the vine: you are the branches; if a man remains in me and I in him. He will bear much fruit. Jesus wants to be as close to you as a branch is to a vine. One is an extension of the other. It is impossible to tell where one starts and the other ends. The branch isn't connected only at the moment of bearing fruit. The gardener doesn't keep branches in a box and then, on the day he wants grapes, glue them to the vine. No, the branch constantly draws nutrition from the vine, because separation means death.

- **A Bride**: What does our marriage to Christ imply? Firstly, the communication never stops. In a happy home a husband doesn't talk to his wife only when he wants something, he doesn't pop in just when he wants a good meal or a clean shirt or a little romance. Healthy marriages have a sense of "remaining". There is tenderness, honesty and ongoing communication. Sometimes we go to God with our joys, with our hurts, but we must always go. The more we go the more we become like him. People who live long together eventually begin to sound alike, talk alike and

54

even think alike. So, the more we walk with Jesus, the more He expects us to take on His principles, His attitude and ultimately His heart.

"By myself I can do nothing; I judge only as I hear, and my judgment is just, for I seek not to please myself but him who sent me". John 5:30.

Studying from the scriptures above, three things are worthy of note in the relationship of Jesus with his father.

- **Intimacy:** *"For the father loveth the son, and sheweth him all things that himself doeth: and he will shew him greater works than these, that ye may marvel" John5:20KJV.* You interact with many people throughout the day, but you only share your heart with those you trust, and with whom you have a close relationship. So how close are you to God right now? Enough to know when you've said or done something which has grieved Him? Enough to feel the warmth of His presence? The truth is you are as close to God as you desire to be, decide to be and discipline yourself to be. Nothing is born unless there is first an act of intimacy between two people/ and intimacy is based on 'desire'. How much do you desire God? Do you desire to earnestly seek Him?
  "O God, thou art my God; early will I seek thee: my soul thirsteth for thee, my flesh longeth for thee in a dry and thirsty land, where no water is". Psalms 63:1. Do you desire His word? *"Neither have I gone back from the commandment of his lips; I have esteemed the words of his mouth more than my necessary food". Job23:12.*

- **Dependency:** *"Then answered Jesus and said unto them, Verily, verily, I say unto you, The Son can do nothing of himself, but what he seeth the Father do: for what things soever he doeth, these also doeth the Son likewise" John5:19KJV.* Jesus knew He couldn't do anything without His father, so He

55

didn't bother to try. Some of us on the other hand, sing, 'Without Him I can do nothing' then go out and act as if everything about our life depends on us. If we succeed, we often become conceited that nobody can stand us. Jesus never struggled with insecurity or battled with fear of failure like we do because it never occurred to Him that He couldn't do something, which His father had already assured Him He could do. Hearing from God enables you to face any obstacles or enemy with confidence. So, before you begin your day, kneel and pray 'Lord I'm counting on you; I don't have a backup plan!'

- **Obedience:** *"I can of mine own self do nothing: as I hear, I judge: and my judgment is just; because I seek not mine own will, but the will of the Father which hath sent me" (John 5:30).* Jesus neither considered nor consulted His own will in the matter. Instead He focused on one thing: doing the will of God. Note the words, 'As I hear'. When you have heard from God, the discussion is over; it's time to act. Making Jesus the Lord of your life, helps you give up three basic rights, and they are: what it will cost you, where it will take you, and the extent to which it will change you. To enjoy a relationship with Jesus similar to the one which He had with His father, is very demanding. Yes, but it's also very protective. When God told his people to do some things, he also told them why; *'Ye shall walk in all the ways which the LORD your God hath commanded you, that ye may live, and that it may be well with you, and that ye may prolong your days in the land which ye shall possess". (Deut5:33). "Hear therefore, O Israel, and observe to do it; that it may be well with thee, and that ye may increase mightily, as the LORD God of thy fathers hath promised thee, in the land that floweth with milk and honey" (Deut. 6:3). "Observe and hear all these words which I command thee, that it may go well with thee, and with thy children after thee for ever, when thou doest that which is good and right in the sight of the LORD thy God". Deut12:28.*
God is not trying to cramp your style, make your life hard or put you in a strait jacket. He is a father who wants only the best for

His children. Isn't that what every good parent wants? So please work in obedience and you will get the best from God.

Four Ways to Build A Relationship with God

1. **Make up Your Mind**: Spiritual growth doesn't happen by osmosis. You don't just wake up with it one morning. You have to set your heart on it and make it your highest priority, otherwise it won't happen. The bible says *"For let not that man supposed that he will receive anything from the Lord; he is a double minded man, unstable in all his ways James1:7-8" (NKJV)*

2. **Break up Your Will:** Until your will is surrendered to God and brought into alignment with his purposes; you will go in circles spiritually. Israel went in circles in the wilderness for forty years, yet they were only eleven miles from the Promised Land. Don't let that happen to you.'' *Now the God of peace, that brought again from the dead our Lord Jesus, that great shepherd of the sheep, through the blood of the everlasting covenant, Make you perfect in every good work to do his will, working in you that which is well pleasing in his sight, through Jesus Christ; to whom be glory for ever and ever. Amen". Hebrews 13:20-21 (KJV)*

3. **Wake up Your Faith**: Obey the leadings of God's Spirit. Don't be afraid, He will not let you down. Just make sure you don't let Him down.'' *But without faith it is impossible to please him: for he that cometh to God must believe that he is, and that he is a rewarder of them that diligently seek him". Hebrews 11:6 KJV.*

4. **Take up Your Cross:** *Then said Jesus unto his disciples, if any man will come after me, let him deny himself, and take up his cross, and follow me.*

For whosoever will save his life shall lose it: and whosoever will lose his life for my sake shall find it. Mathew 16:24-25 KJV.

Before any marriage can be called a good marriage both partners must have made up their mind that no matter what may come their way, separation is not an option. Also, a strong determination to take up your cross is essential to seeing your master at the end of your race.

CHAPTER 7

Celebrate Yourself, Because God Does

"Key to Personal Fulfillment"

Some think so little of themselves that they had rather be in a bad relationship than none at all. Being around people does not guarantee you won't feel lonely. You will end up feeling empty and used, if you hang around the wrong person. Until you overcome your fears of being alone and wait for God to give you the right relationships, you'll continue to feel lonely. Sometimes loneliness is more about not liking yourself than not having people who like you around. Otherwise, why would you spend so much energy avoiding rejection instead of building healthy relationships? Perhaps you think if you don't get involved you won't get hurt. Or you are afraid to open up in case people would criticize you for sharing anything personal. Such anxiety just contributes to your sense of isolation. Motivational speaker Zig Ziglar said, "What you picture in your mind, is what your mind will work on to accomplish. When you change your pictures, you automatically change your performance. So:

1. **You need a true picture of how God sees you**. Paul says, *"Because of what Christ has done we have become gifts... God.... Delights in" (Ephesians 1:11 TLB).*

   "He celebrates and sings because of you, and He will refresh your life with His love." Zephaniah 3:17

2. **You need a true picture of yourself.** David said, *"You.... Put me together inside my mother's body, and I praise you because of the wonderful way you created me. Everything you do is marvelous!" (Psalm 139: 13-14 CEV).*

Having these two pictures clearly in mind stops you from operating with a devalued self-image, and enables you to ask for what you need in a relationship rather than you staying in a lustful and unhealthy relationship that will lead to pain, depression, agony and tears.

If you train yourself to listen carefully to what an individual is saying, he will generally tell you who and what he is before you get into a relationship with him. Prevention is better than cure! More times than not, when someone begins to warn you of his weaknesses and what to expect, you jump in with your motivational "oh no, that can't be true" thoughts, and encourage him to move forward with you. There is a need for you to learn the priceless art of listening without interrupting. If you do, you'll save yourself years of tears, secret disappointments, and negative experiences rather than using your optimism and persuasive style to coerce a person into accepting your goals and objectives. You need to know when a person can't become something just because you want them to or believe they can. They can't run on your fuel! Your character and maturity won't make up for their own lack. Without your awareness of this principle, these high maintenance relationships can weary you and drain your strength for years. In private or professional relationships, if you have to keep motivating to get started, you'll have to keep motivating to maintain people in relationships that make our heads spin and hearts melt as well as those in stable relationships. On the other hand, if you look, listen, pray, and observe, you can decide whether it's worth the effort to engage in the relationship in the first place. God will guide you in this. His Word says, "Look with your eyes…. hear with your ears, fix your mind on everything I show you; for you were brought here…. that I might show them to you".

Essential Ingredients of a Healthy Relationship

1. **Sacrifice:** Sacrifice means something important to you that you give up for some good purpose. Towards my final year at the University, my fiancé (now my husband) proposed that we get married immediately I finished my program. Of course, we had been in courtship for about two years but I was quite young and I had the plans of travelling out of the country, which was a settled issue at home. That would have added another two or

three years to the relationship and my fiancé then was much older than I which meant he was not getting younger. At a point the Holy Spirit ministered to me about sacrifice. Meanwhile my fiancé never mentioned or pressured me again after I had said that the wedding had to wait till after my return from my overseas trip. I later felt I could still travel out any time after my wedding, even though this time around the expenses would not be borne by my father. I made the sacrifice and today I have not regretted it, we have both travelled out of the country over and over again

God had to sacrifice Jesus for the redemption of mankind.

"For God so loved the world that he gave his only begotten Son, that whosoever believeth in him should not perish, but have everlasting life" John3:16

In a healthy relationship, it must not always be about you first.

2.   **Openness:** Openness is the quality of being honest, not keeping secrets and being able to have a heart to heart discussion with your partner without reservation. I learnt of a brother and sister that had already started their courtship, after which they went for general medical test and the lady tested positive to HIV. She told the fiancé after the result was out and the brother said he was still going ahead to marry her, today they are happily married with four kids and none of the children is a carrier. The sister did not cover up; she was open; so the brother could make an informed decision. That is love. Unlike another story I was told where after the marriage, the secret was discovered and the woman said "I was believing God for divine healing and putting my faith to test". That was the reason she kept her HIV status from her fiancé. That was nothing but deceit, you are to disclose your past, present and where you are going (that is the future), and if the person decides to stay and exercise his or her faith with yours, fine, if not then let him/her go. In a relationship where openness

operates, the partners are not deceived, coerced or misled but are allowed to make informed decisions on their own.

I know of another case of a lady that had aborted severally, before going into a relationship she opened up and told the guy her story. The guy told the lady that he would not be able to go ahead with the relationship because his faith was not strong enough to contain such information., To me that is love, because it is not self-seeking.

3. **No Fear in Love:** Fear means to be afraid of someone or something. Maybe you are in a relationship like Sister Tade and Brother John. Anytime Brother John was coming to visit, she was always afraid of what he would say whenever he was around. His reaction and attitude were always unpredictable and always putting her on edge. In such a relationship, you need no one to tell you that there is no true love, because in a healthy relationship you should be able to freely express yourself without fear of what the other party may say or how he would react. Remember the bible says *"There is no fear in love; but perfect love casteth out fear: because fear hath torment. He that feareth is not made perfect in love" (1Jn4:18).* Communication is an adhesive, or glue that holds a relationship together in the midst of their diversity and difficulties.

4. **Trust:** This means to believe that your partner is honest or to have faith in your partner that he /she will not deliberately hurt you. Miss Bola went on excursion with her department while in the university. When she returned after a week, Mr. Jude, her fiancé, asked her how many men slept with her because he did not believe that throughout the one-week no one proposed or had sex with her. This is a relationship that lacks trust and should be discontinued.

I know of another couple; where the husband Mr. Blade was always searching through the wife's (Mrs. Blade's) phone for text messages from other men and she Mrs. Blade was always searching for feminine smell or perfume on the husband's shirt. It is evident that trust is lacking in their marriage.

5. **Commitment:** In a relationship, commitment means you could trust your partner to sincerely stay, hang on and steadfastly stay committed even in adverse situations or unplanned eventualities of life. It also means the determination to work hard and continue to work hard in order to make the relationship better.

    "And, behold, men brought in a bed a man which was taken with a palsy: and they sought means to bring him in, and to lay him before him. And when they could not find by what way they might bring him in because of the multitude, they went upon the housetop, and let him down through the tiling with his couch into the midst before Jesus" (Luke 5:18-19).

    The friends of the paralytic man were truly committed to seeing their friend walk again, so even when the door was blocked and the roof proved an obstacle, they readily surmounted it and eventually brought him before the saviour. Commitment to the relationship on the part of both partners is essential to having a healthy marriage.

6. **Love:** Love in the sense of the word is not only a noun but also a verb, love as a verb is an action word, it can be in the present participle loving and it can also exist in the past as loved, it therefore means that love is not just a name, a feeling or fondness. Love is not selfish, self-centered, or self-gratifying nor fair weather. Love is always there through thick and thin and at all the different seasons of life. Love is not passive; it therefore means responsibility.

"For God so loved the world, that he gave his only begotten Son, that whosoever believeth in him should not perish, but have everlasting life" (John 3:16).

"Above all, love each other deeply, because love covers over a multitude of sins" (1Pet 4:8).

- Dr Paul Brand was a flight surgeon during World War ll. He tells in one of his books of a man named Peter Foster, who was a Royal Air-force (RAF) Pilot. Peter Foster flew a hurricane which was a fighter with a design flaw: the single propeller engine was mounted in the front, and the fuel line ran past the cockpit. In a direct hit, the pilot would instantly be engulfed in flames before he could eject. The consequences were often tragic. Some RAF Pilots caught in that inferno would undergo ten or twenty surgeries to reconstruct their faces. Peter Foster was one of those downed pilots whose faces were burned beyond recognition but had the support of his family and the love of his fiancée. She assured him that nothing had changed except a few millimeters of skin. Two years later they were married. Foster said of his wife, "She became a mirror, she gave me a new image of myself, when I look at her, she gives me a warm, loving smile that tells me I'm okay". Your marriage and other valued relationships in your life ought to work that same way too, even when disfigurement has not occurred. It should be a mutual admiration that builds self-esteem, and overlooks flaws that are not destructive. This kind of commitment is called love.

7. **Affirmation:** This means positive statements asserting the existence of a relationship. It implies therefore that, a relationship which lives in a climate of affirmation creates a greenhouse for growth. Encouraging words, accentuating each other's strength and an attitude that believes the best are all demonstrated through spoken words, notes, gifts and acts of services. The saying holds true: *"Love communicated grows;*

kept within, no one knows!" As you regularly demonstrate affirmation for one another, God's potential for your family becomes a reality! It is never too late.

CHAPTER 8

When There Is a Break
"Go in Peace"

Some breaks are essential and compulsory before some promises of God for our lives can come to pass, some destinies can be fulfilled and certain destinations reached in life. This is not necessarily because those people are bad but due to reasons within or beyond our control or sometimes it may be because you have overstayed your assignment in their lives. So, when such breaks occur, do not fight them or depart in bitterness or hatred.

Biblical and Contemporary Examples

Abraham and Lot
Abraham's late younger brother gave birth to Lot
"Now these are the generations of Terah: Terah begat Abram, Nahor, and Haran; and Haran begat Lot" (Gen. 11:27)

At a point in time Abraham's father, Terah decided to relocate to Canaan, he took Abram, Sarai, (Abram's wife) and Lot his grandson with him, unfortunately he stopped and stayed in Haran where he died.
"And Terah took Abram his son, and Lot the son of Haran his son's son, and Sarai his daughter in law, his son Abram's wife; and they went forth with them from Ur of the Chaldees, to go into the land of Canaan; and they came unto Haran, and dwelt there.
And the days of Terah were two hundred and five years: and Terah died in Haran" (Gen. 11:31-32).

After Terah's death, God appeared to Abram and told him to leave Haran and move on to Canaan. The question here is would it be easy for Abram to leave Lot his nephew behind in Haran while he moved on to Canaan, bearing in mind that they left together with his grandpa Terah? Some instructions from God are sometimes very difficult to carry out but you must always remember that God knows the end from the beginning and He knows the best for us. Also note that to obey is better than sacrifice. Abram decided at the end to take Lot with him.

"So Abram departed, as the LORD had spoken unto him; and Lot went with him: and Abram was seventy and five years old when he departed out of Haran. And Abram took Sarai his wife, and Lot his brother's son, and all their substance that they had gathered, and the souls that they had gotten in Haran; and they went forth to go into the land of Canaan; and into the land of Canaan they came" (Gen. 12:4-5).

Anytime you travel in the company of Lots, it is only a matter of time before trouble, strife, malice, jealousy and envy will set in, due to incompatibility in dreams, vision, goals, desires and aspirations.
"Is not the whole land before thee? Separate thyself, I pray thee, from me: if thou wilt take the left hand, then I will go to the right; or if thou depart to the right hand, then I will go to the left" (Gen13:9).
You must be peaceful especially when you are the Lot that was held onto because of sentiments of how will it feel? What will people say? Because you will need your Abraham several times over.

"And they took Lot, Abram's brother's son, who dwelt in Sodom, and his goods, and departed."
"And when Abram heard that his brother was taken captive, he armed his trained servants, born in his own house, three hundred and eighteen, and pursued them unto Dan."
"And he brought back all the goods, and also brought again his brother Lot, and his goods, and the women also, and the people" (Gen. 14:12, 14, 16).

Abrams must not travel with Lots because of the divine assignment.
"And the LORD said unto Abram, after that Lot was separated from him, Lift up now thine eyes, and look from the place where thou art northward, and southward, and eastward, and westward:
For all the land which thou seest, to thee will I give it, and to thy seed forever.

67

And I will make thy seed as the dust of the earth: so that if a man can number the dust of the earth, then shall thy seed also be numbered. Arise, walk through the land in the length of it and in the breadth of it; for I will give it unto thee" (Gen. 13:14-17).

God did not show Abram the plan for his life until he was separated from lot.

Jonah and the Ship Crew

"Pick me up and throw me into the sea…. And it will become calm" (Jonah 1:12 NIV).

When Jonah boarded a ship going in the opposite direction to God's will, the crew discovered there's a high price to be paid when you allow a wrong person into your life. God hasn't authorized you to be somebody else's life support system, especially if they're running away from Him (God) and if their role in your life is already becoming dangerous. Sometimes you don't want them to leave out of sympathy and they don't want to leave because it's a parasitic relationship where they are the ones benefiting or taking advantage of your magnanimity. When you continue to allow Jonah on board, he will turn your life upside down, and before it's over you are at the risk of losing everything. Why don't you want him to go? Do you seriously think you can fix your Jonah? No, you can't.

"The Lord…. Prepared a great fish to swallow up Jonah!" (Jonah1:17 NIV).

Sometimes the best thing you can do for such a fellow is to wake him up and throw him overboard. "He was sleeping"! [smiling] while you are busy working out your life to rescue the boat [crying]. It may be hard to bear, but more often than not the best thing you can do for your Jonah is to throw him overboard and let God rescue him while you all move on in your different directions in life. Don't because of sympathy force or beg Jonah to stay with you, if you do, you may loose your life and all your valuables in the process.

Orpah and Naomi

"And they took them wives of the women of Moab; the name of the one was Orpah, and the name of the other Ruth: and they dwelled there about ten years.

And Mahlon and Chilion died also both of them; and the woman was left of her two sons and her husband.

Then she arose with her daughters in law, that she might return from the country of Moab: for she had heard in the country of Moab how that the LORD had visited his people in giving them bread.

Wherefore she went forth out of the place where she was, and her two daughters in law with her; and they went on the way to return unto the land of Judah.

And Naomi said unto her two daughters in law, Go, return each to her mother's house: the LORD deal kindly with you, as ye have dealt with the dead, and with me.

The LORD grant you that ye may find rest, each of you in the house of her husband. Then she kissed them; and they lifted up their voice, and wept.

And they said unto her, surely, we will return with thee unto thy people. And Naomi said, turn again, my daughters: why will ye go with me? are there yet any more sons in my womb, that they may be your husbands?

Turn again, my daughters, go your way; for I am too old to have an husband. If I should say, I have hope, if I should have an husband also to night, and should also bear sons;

Would ye tarry for them till they were grown? would ye stay for them from having husbands? nay, my daughters; for it grieveth me much for your sakes that the hand of the LORD is gone out against me.

And they lifted up their voice, and wept again: and Orpah kissed her mother in law; but Ruth clave unto her.

And she said, Behold, thy sister in law is gone back unto her people, and unto her gods: return thou after thy sister in law" (Ruth 1: 4 -15).

Orpah had been married for about ten years to Naomi's son which meant that a sort of relationship would have existed between them [daughter-in-law and mother-in-law]. After they were both bereaved, one of her husbands and the other of her son. The bible records that Ruth and Orpah dealt kindly with Naomi. This further proves that they had a relatively cordial relationship. After some period of time, Naomi decided it was time to leave the land of Moab and go home to Bethlehem, so she advised her two daughters-in-laws to stay behind with their people and she prayed for their future home. They both said they would follow her to her people. On their way, she asked them if they realized that she could not give birth again. Even if she remarried that day and had sons, would they be able to wait till the sons grew into men to marry them? At this point Orpah decided that it was time to go back to Moab to start a new life. Ruth, on her part decided that she would go with Naomi to wherever she went. Naomi's people would be her people and Naomi's God would be her God. Orpah kissed her mother-in-law goodbye. The fact that Orpah kissed Naomi goodbye did not make Orpah a bad person or Ruth a better person. It simply means that Orpah's part in the story of the life of Naomi had ended and there is another part that Ruth had to play in the story of Naomi. Every one of us at one point in time have met people whose love for us seems inseparable but sometimes we can explain and at other times, for reasons we cannot explain they just must leave. We must realize the importance of letting go and allowing such people to leave without being bitter towards them. Don't forget that we meet different people for different reasons; some people appear in our present and their part in our lives ends while some people appear in the present only to re-appear in our tomorrow because their part in the story of our lives is yet to be fully played out. You must recognize when somebody's part in the story of your life has ended, acknowledge that it is over especially after you have tried to make it work. So, joyfully release them and let them go because if you don't, they will rule and lord over you, dictate your life and ultimately make you miserable. So never beg anyone to stay with you no matter the kind of relationship that exists between you and them. When you are in a relationship that you are no longer valued, don't ever be compelled to stay because if you do, it will end in pains, tears and regret.

During my National Youth Service Corps program, I met a colleague of mine who was pregnant as I was, on the first day at the orientation camp we could not complete our registration so we were not entitled to a bed space until the registration was complete. I made up my mind to squat with someone that had completed her registration because I could not go through the stress of collecting the mattress that night to return the following day and still queue for the same mattress when my registration was fully completed. My friend suggested that we should go and collect a single mattress, sleep on it together and return it the next day, so I conceded, unfortunately when we got to the dormitory we discovered that the bed could not accommodate both of us because of our tummies, so I asked her to sleep on it, while I went to squat with a single lady, the next day we both took the mattress with the intention to return it and continue with our registration. The people on the queue that wanted to return their mattress were so many so we decided to go and sit down because of our condition and return it later when the queue had subsided. However, while sitting down with my friend I heard it audibly in my ears, the Holy Spirit asking me to STAND UP! from where I was seated. It was a command. I was still fighting in my spirit man with the command because although we did not use the mattress together eventually, but the intention was for both of us to use it. So, I did not want to leave her alone with the mattress. I heard the same command again STAND UP, so I obeyed. Not up to a minute after I left her, an official of the National Youth Service Corps approached her and said 'Madam you are pregnant!' That was how it started and she was eventually asked to come back for the compulsory one-year programme after delivery. How can I explain my leaving her side? We did not see any official coming. My friend later said maybe I was a witch or had premonition of what was about to happen that day, because my getting away from where we were seated was too timely. What God wanted to achieve was achieved only that we needed a break at that point in time. Even though we were not close friends back in our university days but that incident has brought us together to the extent that today both of us have benefitted and are still benefiting tremendously from the relationship.

Recently, I read in one of the Nigerian dailies, the story of a bank manager who was relieved of her job due to economic situation. She sought greener pasture in the United States, unfortunately because her immigration papers were not complete, she could not get a job of her desire. After some months she settled for a job as a nanny to three children whose parents were also from Nigeria. Unfortunately, she was harassed, threatened and emotionally battered, even her salary was not forth coming as agreed, because her employer oppressed her due to her immigration status. While carrying out her job as a nanny, she injured her big toe. Unfortunately for her she was diabetic, she could not go to the hospital for fear of being repatriated. She called a family friend who encouraged her to leave the job and come to his own state. She eventually left. Few days later, she complained of pain and was persuaded to go to the hospital. After much persuasion, she went, only to be admitted. Few days after, she went into coma and was in this state of comatose for two years before she finally died. I believe she died because she was reluctant to leave both the home where she was living in hell and the country she thought was flowing with milk and honey, when her story in those places had ended.

It should be noted that a break is inevitable in some relationships, so - when a party leaves it is not accidental, it just points to the fact that the purpose for which God brought you together at that particular time had ended, so don't be bitter or leave any relationship in hatred. Always remember that you might need to meet that person in the nearest future. Based on what I now know, I can also make some statements; everything that happens to you, negative or positive, happens to make you what you are, and you should be grateful all the time, even if you don't understand the significance at the moment."

In every situation you find yourself, give thanks, for you do not necessarily have the complete information to conclude that the thing you are complaining about is actually not for your good. Since we don't have complete information, in most cases we tend to complain. Most things happen for our own interest. Whatever negative thing you are facing, the correct action to take is to sit down and address the issue holistically. Pray, make necessary decisions and move on.

Let me share this secret with you and I suggest you learn it by heart. You will only start to really live, the moment you don't rely on what people say or would say to take your decisions. The truth is that the public has no opinion; it is what you eventually do that will form their opinions. If you fail, people will have opinions, and likewise if you succeed, they will also have opinions. That means if your happiness or sadness would depend on how people perceive what you do, then it would be a horrible way to live life.

One of my mentors shared this with me, that at a time when he needed to close a line of business that was not fetching money, he was very concerned about how the public would perceive it. Then one day he just asked himself how many dead bodies would be on the road as a result of closing down the business. Once he found that the answer was that nobody would attribute the death of a person to his closing down of the business, he just shut the business and created another one that has become a phenomenal success. The day you realize that in this journey of life, you are alone, that is the day you start to live. You would be deceiving yourself to imagine that people would take the tough decisions on your behalf. I can only advise you; I can't follow you to where you will execute the decisions. You would be missing out big time in life if you would let what people say influence the actions you would take. Just be fair to other people and get a clearance from your conscience. Move once this is in place. "That is quite instructive" he concluded.

Again, my mentor suggested that you should not be too emotional when you are trying to solve a problem. You should be objective. Get all the facts on the table, seek appropriate counsel and take a decision quickly without emotions. Some of the decisions you would take may not be palatable but you just have to take them and move on.

You should maintain a positive attitude when you are facing a challenge and know that it is a temporary situation that would pass. Again, you should always look for the lessons embedded in every challenge you are facing. There is always something positive you can find in every problem.

So, accept that relationship when it is over because God has something better in stock for you and possibly the other party too. Stop trying to control every possible outcome. Life goes better when you decide to stand on God's Word and trust Him to take care of you. So, trust Him, get up, move on and start living again. Don't forget that the breaks could come from any of the different types of relationships that have been discussed.

The exception to this rule is in marriage, because your parts can never end until you are separated by death. That is why I will advise the singles reading this book to please pray and watch very well before going into marriage and to the married, please, with love and humility, sort out your differences. Remember you have signed and vowed to stay with each other for better or worse. Moreover, God hates divorce!

Here Are Five Ideas for Putting New Life into Your Marriage.
1. **Renew your commitment.** Rough spots are normal in marriage. What else would you expect from two imperfect people? Decide, 'I'm going to win my mate again.' And start with an act of your will, not a feeling in your stomach. Say, 'I'll do what I need to do for the highest good of my mate.' Yes, it is tough only when one partner makes the commitment but when you do, that gets you on track with the Lord and frees Him up to deal with your mate. Any marriage will work when two people say, 'Lord, tell us what to do.' God can make a difference in your marriage, but it takes work. The feeling will come back, but feelings can't be the determining factor in your decision.
2. **Start dating again.** Nobody likes being taken for granted, so, adopt the attitude of 'I'm going to keep wooing and winning my mate.'
3. **Give up something for your mate**. It sends the right signal when you say, 'Yes, I know I planned to do that, but I'd rather be with you.'
4. **Pay attention to little things.** The little stuff gets forgotten too easily, like paying your wife compliments or buying her a card to say 'I love you' or surprising your husband by wearing his favorite shirt and making a special meal.
5. **Accentuate the positive.** Anybody can be a critic. If you look hard enough, you'll never run out of things that aren't perfect about your mate. Try to look hard for something good, let them know what you find, and watch what happens!

Story of The Night by Elvis Grey
When I was a kid, I remember one night in particular when my mom had made dinner after a long, hard day at work. That evening, my Mom

placed a plate of eggs, sausages and extremely burned biscuit in front of Dad. I remember waiting to see if anyone noticed! Yet all Dad did was reached for his biscuit, smiled at Mom and asked me how my day was at school. I don't remember what I told him that night, but I do remember watching him smear butter and jelly on that biscuit and ate every bite!

When I got up from the table that evening, I remember hearing my Mom apologize to my Dad for burning the biscuits. And I'll never forget what he said; "Honey, I love burned biscuits." Later that night, I went to kiss Dad good night and asked him if he really liked his biscuit burned. He wrapped me in his arms and said, "Your Mom put in a hard day at work today and she's really tired, besides a little burned biscuit never hurts anyone!"

Life is full of imperfection and imperfect people. However, what I've learnt over the years is accepting each other's fault and choosing to celebrate each other's differences is one of the most important keys to creating a healthy, growing and lasting relationship without tears.

Advantages of Working Through Your Issues;
- **Emotional Benefits:** contrary to what Hollywood and Nollywood culture will have us believe, divorced people are more likely to feel irrational, aggressive and depressed due to loneliness.
- **Health Benefits:** Emotional stress leads to physical problems and, being in a relationship, especially a good marriage can be beneficial for your health. Relationships help us live longer, improve our happiness and protect us from heart diseases. Regular social contact helps to provide some of the special moments that help to counter stress by supporting us through hard times and acting as a buffer to lessen the burden of personal challenges.
- **Community Benefits:** What your children see influences their future choices. Staying in your marriage teaches them how to work through relationship challenges. Couples with strong marriages helps to build a nation of loving and, responsible parents who can guide their children unto the right track. Author Christi Scannell says, "When my husband and I got married, we agreed it was for life." Weeks before our wedding, we made a pact

to walk out whatever problems came our way! Yes, we could have issues, we could accuse each other, but we won't be moving out or filing papers. Whatever happens, we're staying together!

- Stop trying to control every possible outcome. Life goes better when you decide to stand on God's Word and trust Him to take care of you. [break]

- Loneliness is more about not liking yourself than about not having people around who like you. [stable] [head spin]

- Some people appear in our present and their parts in our life ends while some people appear to re-appear in our tomorrow because their part in the story of our life is not yet over. [Mopelola Arowosafe]. [vital lesson]

- Tough circumstances force you to discover more of your potential. [vital lessons]

- Challenges if properly handled help to sharpen us to be able to handle greater assignment. [break] [vital lessons]

- Everything that happens to you negative or positive happens to make you what you are and you should be grateful all the time, even if you don't understand the significance at the moment. [with God]

- The day you stop learning is the day you start dying. [mentor]

- Be good to everyone you meet because you don't have the full picture of why you are meeting such people. [Mopelola Arowosafe] [fulfill destiny]

- The power of a good relationship is God's blessing for your transition. Mopelola Arowosafe. [God] [mentor]

- You need strategic alliance to fulfill purpose, so learn to differentiate between a good and a bad relationship. [celebrate yourself] [mentor]

- Nothing is born unless there is first an act of intimacy between two people

Chapter 1
Ayo Arowolo, Billionaire's capsules: it is not over until it's over, (Saturday Punch Nig. Ltd, October 10,2009), 52
Ayo Arowolo, Billionaire's capsules: Business and life mistakes to avoid (Saturday Punch Nig. Ltd, February 27, ,2010), 48
Ayo Arowolo, Billionaire's capsule: lesson 10; give thanks always (Saturday Punch Nig. Ltd, November 28, 2009), 50
Ayo Arowolo, Billionaire's capsule: Series 2 lesson 7; focus on the end result (Saturday Punch Nig. Ltd, September 12, 2009), 51

Chapter 3
https://en. m.wikipedia.org>wiki George Washington CARVER In His Own Words GARY R. KREMER 1987

Chapter 5
https://www.investopedia.com>How Aliko Dangote became the richest person in Africa-Investopedia May 2019
https://www.cnbc.com> How Bill Gates and Warren Buffet met, 2017
https://www.legends.report.com>the man who helped Richard Branson 2019
https://abcnews.go.com>story Oprah Winfrey Remembers her mentor Maya Angelou 28 May 2014
https://m.georgiaencyclopedia.orgBenjaminMays(Ca.1894-1984)/NewGeorgia encyclopedia
teamupmentoring.blogspot.com>Darrel Green and his middle school 2015
blog.corporatesufi.com>mentorship/corporatesufi 2018
https://books.google.com.ng>books Bill Russell: A Biography Murry R. Nelson 2005

Chapter 6
Bob and Debby Gass with Ruth Gass Halliday.The Word for Today (June 24,28,2015). (Dec. 14,2011/2012).

Chapter 7
Bob and Debby Gass with Ruth Gass Halliday.The Word for Today (May 12,2015). (July 10 2015).
https://www.rhema.co.nz>item Learning to overlook the flaws -Rhema

Chapter 8
Bob and Debby Gass with Ruth Gass Halliday.The Word for Today (March 28,2010). (Nov 29,31,2010)
Jebose I. rssing.com>latest The Punch- Nigeria's most widely read. NewsPaper >> Jebose Boulevard

ACKNOWLEDGEMENTS

I first got the inspiration to write this book about four years ago but due to several distractions I kept leaving it on my table uncompleted and unpublished. In January 2019 the Holy Spirit gave me a push towards writing the book again. At the same time, the date for the launching dropped in my heart to immortalize my son's name and to celebrate the anniversary of his transition to glory. Oreoluwa Oluwakayode Oluwatimilehin became the young donkey that was ridden to heaven by Jesus and became one of the young that was mentioned in the book of Revelation. Though his stay was short, his life was meaningful and his faith was firm in Christ to the very end. We love him and we can never forget him.

To this end we want to specially appreciate those people who stood by our family in their own little way by their act of kindness. To my God who has forever been on my side, my Father, my strength and my anchor when the billows roll. Thank you, Daddy, for the privilege to know you and for having a very deep relationship with me.

Engr. and Mrs Michael Kehinde, Dr and Mrs Timothy Adeyemo, Tosin Adepoju, Engr and Mrs Abiodun fijabi, Pastor and Mrs D.G Adeyemi (CAC), RCCG Jesus The Light Family, Abeokuta, I say a big Thank you, God will not forget your labour of love in Jesus name.

RCCG Agape Mega Parish Family Abeokuta, even though we were no longer there as their pastors, the encouragement was overwhelming. Letters of hope_org, I love the pillow with the Word of God printed on it, God bless your ministry and organization. Pastor Bisi Adewale, Pastor and Pastor {Mrs} I. O Abatan, (Retired Director General of the Directorate of Christian Education Worldwide, member board of trustees of the Redeemed Christian Church of God), you are fathers and a mother indeed. Pastor and Pastor {Mrs} Gbadebo Emehinola (PICP

Ogun 6), their assistants and their wives, RCCG Ogun Province 6 Admin and Account staffs. Pastor {Mrs} Olori Bimpe Lipede, Pastor {Mrs} Kemi Abiodun (WPICP, RCCG Ogun 1), Pastor and Pastor {Mrs} Timothy Olaniyan (PICP, RCCG Lagos Province 12), Pastor and Pastor {Mrs} Olusola John (PICP RCCG, Ogun Province 11), Assistant pastor and {Mrs} E.O Akinbo, your presence was highly encouraging, I say, thank you.

Our neighbours, families, friends, spiritual children, and several people too numerous to mention. Those who contributed to the writing of this book, Architect Femi Sowande, Barr. Dotun Sotonade, Yemi Odetola, Thanks for making this book readable, God bless you dear ones. Dr Dele Odunlami, Mrs Ademilola Adesanya, Pastor [Mrs] Mosun Aiyanyo, Prof [Mrs] Fapojuwo, Dr [Mrs] Itunu Folarin- for your encouragement, selflessness and professionalism in reading, and editing the manuscript, though the time was short, thank you all. Ibukunoluwa and Atinuke, though you wept because Oreoluwa was indeed an example of a good big brother to you both, but you took it in good faith, you will never shift your gaze from the master, you will both get there in all areas of life in Jesus name. I love you both.

My Crown, I am the only one that can understand how you feel about your exact copy, it is well and it will keep getting well in the real sense of it. We have come this far by His love. Farther and further we shall go together by His undeserved grace on our lives. I love you.

We pray that whatever be the type of relationship between us it will keep getting better, and stronger. The Arowosafes love you all.

Mopelola Arowosafe is an international teacher of the word, an intentional living coach, a bible coach, an inspirational speaker, a passionate and seasoned marriage counselor and author of the bestselling book "Keys to a fulfilling Marriage''. She is the founder of Intending Couple's Class {ICC} an interdenominational couples' class that has produced many couples with testimonies of good homes. She is equally the founder of the Lineage of Grace, a mentoring group on social media, where the scriptures that talk about females in the bible are systematically studied from Genesis to Revelation amongst several women across different cultures, age group and countries.

She is currently the Treasurer of the Association of Nigerian Authors (ANA) Ogun State Branch.

She holds a Bachelor of Science degree in Food Science and Technology, Diploma degrees in Discipleship, Theology and

Missions all from the Redeemed Christian Bible College and School of Missions respectively.

She is happily married to Adekunle Arowosafe, an architect, a teacher of the word, Her Crown and a Senior Pastor with the Redeemed Christian Church of God. They are blessed with children and live in Abeokuta Ogun state, Nigeria.

You can reach the author through

Keystoafullfillingmarriage@gmail.com or arowosafemopelola@yahoo.com

Follow me on Instagram: @keystoafulfillingmarriage (Mopelola Arowosafe)

Follow me on Facebook at Mopelola Arowosafe and Arowosafe Mopelola

Follow me on WhatsApp and Telegram at 08062296041

Call me on +234 806 229 6041, 808 087 6130

Printed in Great Britain
by Amazon